Women With Influence

WOMEN WITH INFLUENCE

HOW 12 LEADING WOMEN BUILT A SUCCESSFUL WORLD-CLASS CORPORATE CONSULTING PRACTICE

Jane Anderson

Editing: Kristen Lowrey

Typeset by BookPOD

ISBN: 978-0-6480489-8-5 (pbk)
eISBN: 978-0-6480489-9-2 (ebook)

NATIONAL LIBRARY OF AUSTRALIA

A catalogue record for this book is available from the National Library of Australia

To Lillian Armfield; the trailblazer and pathfinder.

For reminding us that we all have the ability to have more influence than we think.

ABOUT THE AUTHOR

Jane Anderson is a strategic communications expert and is passionate about working with women in consulting. She has over 20 years' experience in corporate communications and capabilities, and she has worked with over 100,000 people to elevate their influence in their businesses and careers.

Jane has recently been voted as one of the top three branding gurus globally. She has won more than 25 marketing, sales and communication awards and also has one of the top 1% most viewed LinkedIn profiles.

She is the host of the iTunes podcast *The Jane Anderson Show*, and has achieved acclaim interviewing thought leaders and experts such as Seth Godin. Jane has also been featured in *Business Insider*, *Sky Business*, the *Sydney Morning Herald* and *The Age*, and she is a contributor on *Forbes*.

Her clients include some of the world's leading experts in their field, as well as iconic brands such as Virgin Australia, Lego, Ikea, Rio Tinto and Origin Energy.

Jane is also dedicated to helping female consultants position and promote themselves, and ensure that they're charging what they're worth. She has built (and continues to build) a diverse group of like-minded female industry leaders who support and help each other grow their practices.

Obsessed with elevating influence in all areas, Jane is the author of nine books, speaks at conferences and delivers group and one-on-one mentoring to consultants looking to grow their practices. She lives in Brisbane, Australia with her husband Mark and stubborn English Bulldog, Winston.

ACKNOWLEDGEMENTS

At school I had an amazing business studies teacher called Mr Benfield. In fact, he was exceptional. He was kind, creative and quirky. I'm not a very competitive person but he seemed to bring out this side in me – one that I didn't even know I had. His teaching motivated and inspired me.

What made him unique was that he was a hippie. This was in a small country town in northern NSW, so it wasn't a big deal at all. But to have a hippie for a *business* teacher was pretty unique.

There was something else that made him better than other teachers – he used to set me reading assignments so that I could work ahead. I loved the subject, and when he saw that, he found expansion work for me to read in the textbook. On one occasion he even set me the task of teaching a lesson on vertical and horizontal integration to the entire class.

Mr Benfield knew how to cultivate my interest and get the most out of me. No other teacher that I had ever experienced was able to make a subject interesting enough to inspire me.

It became my best subject at school and, as a result, I decided to study business at university. I wanted to become a business studies teacher myself. Ultimately, I became a business coach instead of a teacher, but it was Mr Blenfield who helped me to realise what I loved and inspired me to follow a career in this space.

I've been fortunate to have some exceptional people in my life along with Mr Benfield who have inspired this book.

I will always be indebted to Matt Church for harnessing my thinking.

To the masters of their craft and my masterminds – Rowdy McLean, Keith Abraham, Amanda Stevens, Andrew Griffiths, Emma McQueen and Belinda Brosnan who have

Acknowledgements

had such an impact on every idea in this book and pushed me far beyond what I could have achieved on my own. This would not have happened without you.

To the clients that I work with every day and who work on every aspect of this book in their practices – you are such an inspiration with the ripple you create in the world. I am grateful to see the work behind the scenes and admire how you constantly grapple with your ideas, messaging and positioning in order to make a difference on the planet.

To the team closest to me who make projects like this come to life. My husband Mark, who is one of the smartest and kindest human beings on the planet. His support along with my family has been unconditional. The late night proofreading and listening ear has been beyond invaluable. Thank you for your patience and making this come to life.

To my support team in the office, MC and Monique, who share the vision to create change, educate, innovate and help people grow their practices so they can have a greater impact in the world. Thank you for your hard work and looking after everything else so that I can get books like this completed!

Finally to my editor, Kristen Lowrey, and publisher, Sylvie Blair at BookPOD. Thank you for your commitment and dedication and being part of the team for every book project to date. Without you these ideas don't see the light of day.

Jane

CONTENTS

CHAPTER 1

WHY WOMEN IN CORPORATE CONSULTING MATTER

'A woman with a voice by definition is a strong woman. But the search to find that voice can be remarkably difficult.'

– Melinda Gates

Today's women in consulting are battling the perfect storm. The world is changing. The world of work is changing. The role of women at work is changing. Business growth is changing. Consulting is changing. Even our clients' problems are changing.

All of these changes mean that women in corporate consulting matter more than ever. This age of disruption is creating paths for female experts to make change and create impact to truly become women with influence.

What's Happening in the World

The COVID-19 pandemic has had a widespread and far-reaching impact on the world. As part of this it has also significantly changed the global work environment. The pandemic accelerated existing trends that were already on the rise, such as remote work, e-commerce and automation. Companies that were already exploring these changes and advancing these technologies were forced to rapidly accelerate new behaviours. Companies that hadn't yet begun that transition were forced to rapidly adopt new behaviors. And, in all cases, researchers believe that these new behaviours are here to stay[1]. In fact, today more that 40% of Australians work from home. For those in the professional fields, it's up to 64%.[2]

We've also been experiencing what has been called the 'war for talent'. This is a term coined by Steven Hankin of McKinsey & Company in 1997, and clarified in the book, *The War for Talent* by Ed Michaels, Helen Handfield-Jones and Beth Axelrod. The term refers to the increasing competition to recruit and retain high-performing employees.[3] Combined with the 'great resignation' – the notion that record numbers have or will leave their jobs after the pandemic ends[4] – and society is left struggling to keep the workforce humming along while we're left struggling to find and keep a really good team. People today are no longer content to stay in a job just because it pays the bills. Instead, they're looking to be happy and fulfilled, and to do what they love.

Another change in the world has been our ability to access our own publishing platforms. We're no longer limited by the attention we can get through traditional media or marketing (such as paid TV or radio spots). We can make our own media. There are social media platforms, of course. But you can also write your own book, record a podcast or even create your own TV show. These platforms are free (or very low cost) and they've significantly levelled the playing field for small and medium businesses and consulting practices.

Flexibility, a desire and a route to do what you love, a workforce that can create their own platforms – all of these have combined to change the way that business works today. And these changes have opened the door to more opportunities for women in consulting.

---

1   McKinsey & Company. (18 February 2021). 'The future of work after COVID-19'. [Report]. Accessed at https://www.mckinsey.com/featured-insights/future-of-work/the-future-of-work-after-covid-19.

2   Australian Bureau of Statistics. (14 December 2021). 'More than 40 per cent of Australians worked from home.' [Press Release]. Accessed at https://www.abs.gov.au/media-centre/media-releases/more-40-cent-australians-worked-home.

3   Michaels, E., Handfield-Hones, H. and Axelrod, B. (2001). *The War for Talent*. Harvard Business Press. Accessed at https://books.google.com.au/books?id=simZCd_YUC4C&redir_esc=y.

4   Chugh, A. 'What is 'The Great Resignation'? An expert explains.' 29 November 2021. World Economic Forum. Accessed at https://www.weforum.org/agenda/2021/11/what-is-the-great-resignation-and-what-can-we-learn-from-it/.

Business Growth in a Social-First World

In 2020-21 the number of small businesses with employees had increased by nearly 15% from just three years previous.[5] And much of this is down to the way that businesses grow in the modern world.

Business growth today works quite differently to how it used to work years ago. It used to be about cold-calling, sales demonstrations and qualifying leads. But today it's all about engaging and educating your audiences, either via social media or through non-traditional media outlets, such as podcasting.

Today, rather than cold calling, sales demos and leads, we're now utilising educational and engaging content that we share through our social and non-traditional media channels. And the data shows that this works. In fact, content that educates increases engagement by a whopping 83.6% [6]. That's a big jump, and a big way to get attention. It's also an excellent way to prove to your audience that they can trust you to bring value into their world. As Seth Godin says, 'The world doesn't need more cat videos'. What the world needs is change, and it's our job as women with influence, to give voice to that.

The Rise of Women

We often hear quotes that highlight gender disparity.

> *Decades ago, Bull, Southey and Tamahori (1979, 41) predicted that the Australian companies that acted to address the needs of disadvantaged groups (including women) would 'fare best during the next decade of social change'. And yet, not long after the enactment of Australia's 1986 Affirmative Action (Equal Employment Opportunity for Women) Act, Kramar (1988, 32) described Australia's progress toward gender equality as 'two steps forward, one step back'. Twenty years later, despite the*

---

5   Australian Government, Business. (15 February 2022). 'Business trends for 2022.' Accessed at https://business.gov.au/news/business-trends-for-2022.

6   Stebbins, C. 'Educational Content Makes Consumers 131% More Likely to Buy.' 6 July 2017. Conductor Spotlight. Accessed at https://www.conductor.com/blog/2017/07/winning-customers-educational-content/.

1999 Equal Opportunity for Women in the Workplace Act, Knox (2008, 153) characterised women's progress in the Australian labour market as 'disappointing'. Voicing the question that scholars have been asking for decades, Evans and Maley (2021, 204) recently wondered why 'Australian corporations are not doing more to progress gender balance in senior leadership'.[7]

And it's true that a gender pay gap (about 14%) still exists in Australia.[8] Even more tellingly, currently only 33 of the Fortune 500 companies are led by female CEOs demonstrating a massive gender gap at the senior executive levels.[9]

This is painting a pretty dreary picture for women in business. Yet, when you look at the bigger picture, we see a slightly different view. We get an incredible view of women on the rise.

Women on the rise worldwide

Worldwide women are gaining a bigger voice, a greater power and more exposure – even in some of the world's most restrictive countries. In Saudi Arabia, women have been given the right to drive.[10] While this may not seem like a big step forward to those of us in Western countries, this was a move that 'cracked open a window to new freedoms for women that have long lived under oppressive laws'.[11]

---

7   Kulik, C. 'Gender (in)equality in Australia: good intentions and unintended consequences.' 30 September 2021. Asia Pacific Journal of Human Resources. Accessed at https://onlinelibrary.wiley.com/doi/10.1111/1744-7941.12312?af=R.

8   Australian Government, Workplace Gender Equality Agency. (8 March 2022). 'Australia's Gender Pay Gap Statistics.' Accessed at https://www.wgea.gov.au/publications/australias-gender-pay-gap-statistics.

9   Zillman, C. 'The Fortune 500 Has More Female CEOs Than Ever Before.' 16 May 2019. Fortune. Accessed at https://fortune.com/2019/05/16/fortune-500-female-ceos/.

10 Momtaz, R. 'Saudi women get behind the wheel of a car for the first time in history'. 24 June 2018. ABC News. Accessed at https://abcnews.go.com/International/saudi-women-wheel-car-time-history/story?id=56097713.

11 Specia, M. 'Saudi Arabia Granted Women the Right to Drive. A Year on, It's Still Complicated.' 24 June 2019. The New York Times. Accessed at https://www.nytimes.com/2019/06/24/world/middleeast/saudi-driving-ban-anniversary.html#:~:text=Saudi%20Arabia%20granted%20women%20the%20right%20to%20drive%20one%20year,long%20lived%20under%20repressive%20laws.

Worldwide there are more women in politics and in leadership positions. You just have to look at the state of Queensland which – for the first time in history – has a female Governor, Premier, Chief Justice and Police Commissioner.[12] And there are more and more women entering politics. In the latest federal election, there were more women than ever chosen to represent their electorates, most of them ousting conservative male counterparts.[13] There has been a rise of funding and grants for women-oriented projects, and we can expect to see even more under our new Labour Government.[14]

Importantly, we see women gaining their voice and embracing their value. Fantastic examples of these are Grace Tame[15] and Brittany Higgins[16] – incredible advocates for survivors of sexual assault. They are using their voices and their platforms to drive cultural and structural change, with the ultimate goal of a future free from the sexual abuse of children and women.

And we're seeing women embracing their value as they age as well, knowing that what they have to offer doesn't start and stop with motherhood (as it would have traditionally). We see this with Demi Moore who posed naked for the cover of Harper's

12 Bita, N. 'Qld's top women speak out.' 28 May 2022. The Courier Mail. Accessed at https://www.couriermail.com.au/subscribe/news/1/?sourceCode=CMWEB_WRE170_a_GGL&dest=https%3A%2F%2Fwww.couriermail.com.au%2Flifestyle%2Fweekend%2Fi-was-the-only-woman-so-i-was-given-the-coffee-order-qlds-top-women-speak-out%2Fnews-story%2F20563648e1e0f075674f72db14c67fdc&memtype=anonymous&mode=premium&v21=dynamic-cold-control-score&V21spcbehaviour=append.

13 Nobel, F. 'Record number of women elected to Australian parliament.' 26 May 2022. 9News. Accessed at https://www.9news.com.au/national/federal-election-2022-record-number-of-women-elected-to-parliament/3ab3b8ea-1e5f-4e11-b3b2-e9f35903c186.

14 Australian Government, Department of the Prime Minister and Cabinet. (8 September 2022). 'Funding for six projects to boost women's employment and leadership'. [Press Release]. Accessed at https://ministers.pmc.gov.au/gallagher/2022/funding-six-projects-boost-womens-employment-and-leadership.

15 Mullins, S. 'Grace Tame recalls moment she confronted her abuser days before she reported him to police'. 9 March 2022. ABC News. Accessed at https://www.abc.net.au/news/2022-03-09/grace-tame-recalls-the-moment-she-confronted-her-abuser/10089551.

16 Karp, P. 'Brittany Higgins rape charge: Bruce Lehrmann to stand trial in June'. 18 November 2021. The Guardian. Accessed at https://www.theguardian.com/australia-news/2021/nov/18/brittany-higgins-charge-bruce-lehrmann-to-stand-trial-in-june.

Bazaar in 2019 at the age of 56[17]. And May Musk who was recently featured on the cover of Sports Illustrated – at the beautiful age of 74[18].

But it's not enough.

The Future of Women in Consulting

Our future – as female consultants – is dependent on our ability to rise as women. And this book is part of that process. Now is the perfect time to become a woman of influence – and to focus on growing your consulting practice to help more people in the world, because the world needs more female consultants.

In fact, there are a tremendous number of benefits that prove why women in consulting matter. First, women leaders and experts bring something unique to the workplace and to the world. Research shows they bring a unique transformational viewpoint[19] while also enhancing teamwork. They also rank better on superior leadership traits[20] and gender-diverse workforces are statistically more profitable[21]. Importantly, research also demonstrates that women leaders provide better mentorship[22], and this is a vital component of continuing to bring women forward into their own power in the workplace and in the world.

17 'Demi Moore strips down for Harper's Bazaar cover'. [Video]. 12 September 2019. USA TODAY. Accessed at https://www.usatoday.com/videos/entertainment/celebrities/2019/09/12/demi-moore-bares-all-harpers-bazaar-cover/2302205001/.

18 Orie, A. 'Maye Musk becomes oldest Sports Illustrated Swimsuit cover model'. 18 May 2022. CNN Style. Accessed at https://edition.cnn.com/style/article/maye-musk-sports-illustrated-swimsuit-intl-scli/index.html.

19 Eagly, A., Makhijani, M. and Klonsky, B. (1992). 'Gender and the Evaluation of Leaders: A Meta-Analysis.' American Psychological Association. Accessed at http://mlkrook.org/pdf/Eagly_1992.pdf.

20 Pew Research Center. (25 August 2008). 'Men or Women: Who's the Better Leader? A Paradox in Public Attitudes.' Accessed at https://www.pewresearch.org/social-trends/2008/08/25/men-or-women-whos-the-better-leader/.

21 Workplace from Meta. '7 benefits of gender diversity in the workplace.' Accessed at https://www.workplace.com/blog/diversity-in-the-workplace?t=b.

22 Ziv, S. '7 Striking Facts About the State of Women in the Workplace.' The Muse. Accessed at https://www.themuse.com/advice/7-striking-facts-women-in-the-workplace-2018.

Challenges keep the pressure on to think small

Of course, women in consulting are still facing challenges. Many of us are struggling to balance it all – family, friends, outside responsibilities plus running a busy practice keeps us extremely time poor. And we struggle with many of the things that women in any business struggle with, such as imposter syndrome, unsupportive partners, pricing, cash flow and financial management challenges, as well as finding ways to elevate our business acumen.

These challenges continue to put pressure on women in consulting to *think small*. To not try to move outside of our comfort zone, or to make innovations or challenges to the status quo.

This is demonstrated by the serious underrepresentation of women on the stage – presenting their well-earned thought leadership to the world. In fact, women come in at an abysmal 32% of speakers at professional events.[23] This not only keeps our thoughts and innovations in our own heads – rather than out in the world – but also means that those thoughts are being replaced, almost across the board, by the thought leadership of our male counterparts.

Women are also underrepresented in the media for the same (or similar) reasons. Susan Byrnes, Chief Communications Officer for the Bill & Melinda Gates Foundation, says that 'Women are vastly underrepresented in news headlines' with 'the voice of every woman drowned out by up to six men'.[24] This is a worldwide phenomenon. Though women make up half the population, they only make up 39% of journalists. They're quoted only 29% of the time in news stories. And this was the highest percentage – in the UK. In other countries it's much lower.[25]

This underrepresentation of women 'in power' or in positions typically held by men is endemic. So prevalent that we don't even see it. In 2005, Lawrence Summers, then president of Harvard, said that women were poorly represented in science because

---

23 Galvez, B. 'New Study: Almost Two-Thirds of Professional Event Speakers Are Male'. 18 December 2019. Bizzabo. Accessed at https://www.bizzabo.com/blog/event-gender-diversity-study-2019/.

24 Byrnes, S. 'Missing Perspectives: How women are left out of the news'. 2 December 2020. Goalkeepers. Accessed at https://www.gatesfoundation.org/ideas/articles/women-in-media-report.

25 Byrnes. Missing Perspectives.

they didn't have the same natural ability to do mathematics that men did.[26] While this caused a nationwide uproar, it demonstrates the perspective that existed less than 17 years ago. And why it's so easy for women today to continue to be impacted by a feeling of being less than.

Women still think they need to seek permission to strive forward. But as Patti Fletcher, gender equality advocate and author of *Disrupters: Success Strategies from Women Who Break the Mold*, says, 'seeking permission gives away your power to disrupt and innovate.'[27] Instead, we need to meet these challenges head on by finding our community, embracing our uniqueness and stepping into our own sphere of influence.

If we keep moving along the trajectory that we're currently on, it will take 170 years for women to achieve economic parity on a worldwide scale.[28] But as women with influence we can do a lot to ensure it takes much less time. Together we can bash through that glass ceiling, not only by becoming leaders and experts in our niche, but also by bringing other women along with us.

The women featured in this book are here because they're doing just that. They're making inroads, and creating bigger and better opportunities for other women. They're not just successful in their own practices, or experts in their own niche, but they're also mentoring and motivating to change the world as part of our Women with Influence Community and through their own communities. And this change is a wonderful thing!

We look forward to introducing you to each and every one of them. They will truly show you why women in consulting matter.

---

26 Acker, J. (2006). 'Inequality Regimes: Gender, Class, and Race in Organizations'. Gender and Society. Accessed at https://journals.sagepub.com/doi/abs/10.1177/0891243206289499.

27 Fletcher, P. 'Wonder Women: Don't Ask for Permission to Make Big Moves'. 11 October 2017. Entrepreneur. Accessed at https://www.entrepreneur.com/leadership/wonder-women-dont-ask-for-permission-to-make-big-moves/302355.

28 World Economic Forum. (30 March 2021). Global Gender Gap Report 2021. [Report] Accessed at https://www.weforum.org/reports/global-gender-gap-report-2021/.

🔑 Key Questions

1. Where are you in your consulting practice journey?
2. What do you think a consulting practice will give you over any other type of business or job?
3. How will your consulting practice help you to mentor or motivate other women?
4. What steps can you take to become a woman with influence?

CHAPTER 2

12 BARRIERS FOR WOMEN BUILDING A CONSULTING PRACTICE

'In the middle of every difficulty lies an opportunity.'

– Albert Einstein

Many years ago, I divorced and started life over again. I decided to give myself five years on my own to build my business and focus on what I needed before getting back out in the dating world.

Once I was back to a level of independence, I decided to start dating again. It was hard – so much had changed. How people meet had changed. How they communicated had changed. I was also older and, suddenly, I felt a bit washed up. Admittedly, I was only 39, but I don't think I've met anyone who hasn't been daunted by the experience of putting themselves out there again.

I think some of the women in consulting clients I work with feel the same way when it comes to building and growing their consulting practice. They don't want to seem pushy or salesy so they struggle to sell and generate revenue. They worry about the tall poppy syndrome so they struggle to be the face in their content. And they grapple with imposter syndrome, which makes unpacking their expertise and knowledge (hard won and brilliant as it is!) quite daunting.

Of course, there's a huge element of vulnerability that goes with sharing what you think, whether you send it out to the public in a newsletter or post it online. It looks easy until it comes time to do it. Then many women can hit a wall of self-doubt, avoidance and fear. They worry they won't be good enough or that they don't have the time. In fact, they can create endless excuses and fears that hold them back from being fully self-expressed.

Having your own consulting practice is a vulnerable game to play and, yes, I was in the same boat when I started, just as I had been when I'd gotten back into the dating world after my divorce. I questioned who would listen to me, if I was relevant and what I could possibly share that hadn't been shared before. But once you know how to overcome these barriers to starting it's like turning on a tap – the ideas start pouring out and a weight lifts off your shoulders.

Having helped people start and grow their corporate consulting practices for more than 10 years, and writing my own blog for the previous 10, I have found people commonly face very similar barriers or challenges when starting their own consulting practice. Overcoming these is the secret to moving forward into success.

12 Barriers for Women Building a Consulting Practice

Barrier 1: My Ideas Aren't Good Enough.

Everyone faces the challenge of feeling like an imposter – even the most seasoned experts and content creators. The thing to remember is that everybody else is afraid of the same thing. So you have a massive advantage if you face this challenge head-on and take action. Because if you don't, the consequence is inertia, which means nothing changes. You will continue to feel like your ideas aren't good enough, that your accomplishments come from luck and that you're a fraud. And that will stop you from creating content.

One of my clients, Jess, went through the same experience. Jess was a young mum who felt like she could help people. But she wasn't sharing her ideas. She was just order-taking in her practice and giving people what they asked for. She was a clever marketer but she didn't think her ideas were good enough. She felt like an imposter. But once Jess unpacked her ideas and started sharing, she got swamped! In fact, she became so busy, she had to force her prices up. She even won an entrepreneurship award!

Author Maya Angelou once said, 'I've written eleven books, but each time, I think, uh-oh, they're going to find me out now. I've run a game on everyone and they're going to find me out.'

Even the most successful people feel this sometimes. But pushing past it is vital for success.

Overcoming This Barrier

So, how do you overcome this fear? Well, you need to do the work. You need to start writing and creating. Start unpacking your ideas. Get your knowledge out of your head and onto paper. It will feel scary at first but the more you create, the more you build your confidence. And the more you build your confidence, the more content you will create. It's a beautiful cycle that will see you overcoming your fear.

Barrier 2: Everything Has Been Said. I Have Nothing To Add.

You may be operating in exactly the same space as someone else. You may have very similar offerings. And you may find that you have a lot of competitors. But you should never feel like you have nothing to add. Because the difference here is you.

You have a different worldview, different experiences and different knowledge. You, as a person, are completely unique. And the context you operate in is completely different to everyone else's. This perspective adds substance and insight to anything that you have to say, even if you're saying things that others have 'already said'.

When you think you have nothing to add, it's like handbag designer Kate Spade saying, 'Well, there are already all these handbags out in the world, what value could I bring?' Tell me, what woman wouldn't want a new handbag just because she already has one!

What's more, if you look at the amount of content people are creating, it's quite small. On LinkedIn, for example, only about 1% of people are creating content, even though LinkedIn sessions increase 25% each year.[1] And the research confirms that we're consuming more content than we are producing, especially in Australia.[2] The market hasn't been able to keep up because people are looking for experts to solve their problems.

Overcoming This Barrier

Don't become someone who isn't meeting the demand for thought leadership. The space is there. People are consuming content. But they can't consume yours if it isn't out there. Focus on what you need to do. Stop looking at everybody else and focus on your clients, your tribe and being their leader.

Barrier 3: What if I Get Trolled?

The word 'troll', which comes from a fishing term, is internet slang for somebody who starts arguments or upsets or harasses people by posting off-topic or extraneous messages. They're like a school bully – they might be picking on you, but what they want is attention.

Huffington Post recently shared some research that said of 1,125 adults, 28% admitted to malicious online activity directed at somebody they didn't know.[3] My experience has been that it's much less than this. Perhaps these results were due to a high volume of bullies in a particular group?

I do love this quote from stand-up comedian Dane Cook. 'Trolls look for reasons to hate but really what they are mad at is the fact they are not included in anything ever.'

---

1   Osman, M. "Mind-Blowing LinkedIn Statistics and Facts (2022)". 20 May 2022. KINSTA BLOG. Accessed at https://kinsta.com/blog/linkedin-statistics/#:~:text=Content%20Creators%20Make%20 Use%20of%20LinkedIn&text=But%20only%20around%203%20million,net%20the%209%20 billion%20impressions.

2   Yellow Social Media Report 2020. Part One - Consumers. 2020. Accessed at https://2k5zke3drtv7fuwec1mzuxgv-wpengine.netdna-ssl.com/wp-content/uploads/2020/07/ Yellow_Social_Media_Report_2020_Consumer.pdf.

3   Kleinman, A. "28 Percent Of Americans Admit To Being Internet Trolls". 20 October 2014. *Huffington Post*. Accessed at https://www.huffpost.com/entry/internet-trolls-survey_n_6014826.

Overcoming This Barrier

Most of the time, it's generally best to ignore the trolls or try not to show you care. Their behaviour says more about them than it does about you. And there's really nothing you can say or do to stop trolls. Just remember, that the people that matter will see them for who they are.

Barrier 4: Fear of Being Boring

The reality is, most people share this fear. No one wants to be boring. The key is to stay visible and know how to add value for your audience.

Saying you don't want to be boring, so you just won't share content, is a bit like saying, 'I don't want to go to the supermarket, so I just won't eat'.

The best thing about regularly sharing your expertise is that it becomes part of your every day. It also validates other people. By seeing and hearing from you frequently, by being part of your every day, your audience gets to see the real you – not just the best bits, but your authentic self. This enables them to relate to you more, and they start to connect with you at a human level. And when they know the real you, it is anything but boring.

Overcoming This Barrier

The only real way to overcome the fear of being boring is to just get started. Share your everyday situations – but also make sure you share your insights. Some days you might create a post, or write an article, that just hits it out of the park, really conveying your thought leadership and driving engagement. And some days you might not have that experience. That's perfectly normal and is par for the course with social media use. But as long as you're saying *something* (and that something adds value) then you're on the right path.

Justin Timberlake once said, 'The most boring thing in the world? Silence'. So, the more frequently you can create, the less boring you will be!

And remember, people connect with real, not perfect. Engage with your audience by asking questions, creating videos, using memes or creating a podcast with your content. There are so many different ways to engage people. The only way you'll bore people is by saying nothing – or sharing cat videos or photos of your food every day!

Barrier 5: I Don't Know How to Use Technology

Great. You're not the only one. Technology changes every day on some platforms. As soon as I wrote my book, *Connect*[4], about LinkedIn, it was out of date. The goal is to stay in your genius – you're not a technology expert, and you don't have to be.

But working with some technology can make you feel like you're in a foreign country. It's like a completely new language that you have to re-learn all the time. George Couros, author of *The Innovator's Mindset*[5], said, 'Technology will not replace great teachers, but technology in the hands of great teachers can be transformational.'[6] And it can become an excellent tool for you to spread your message and run your practice.

Overcoming This Barrier

Using technology as a leader to inspire and communicate with people, and to lead them through change, is truly transformational. Don't let it overwhelm you. When you're starting with any new technology, just keep it simple. Elicit help from administrative staff or others in your organisation, or onboard a virtual assistant if you're running your own business. There are experts in technology that can help you use it to your advantage.

Barrier 6: I Don't Know What to Share

One of the challenges that many women in consulting face is that they don't know what to share. The reality is, you have great ideas all the time. You know how to solve

---

4   Anderson, J. and Chown, K. (2015). Connect: Leverage your LinkedIn Profile for Business Growth and Lead Generation in Less Than 7 Minutes Per Day. Jane Anderson P/L.

5   Couros, G. (2015). The Innovator's Mindset: Empower Learning, Unleash Talent, and Lead a Culture of Creativity. Dave Burgess Consulting, Inc.

6   Couros, G. [@gcouros]. (12 September 2014). Technology will never replace great teachers, but technology in the hands of a great teacher can be transformational. [Tweet]. Twitter. Accessed at https://twitter.com/gcouros/status/510094558320152576?lang=en.

your clients' problems. Your solutions are perfectly designed just for them. You just need to capture these ideas and solutions.

I remember when I felt like I didn't have anything to share and didn't know what to create. But then I followed the very simple process of writing my ideas down. Every time I had a thought or a notion about my practice and my content, I wrote it down. Over time, it became a habit, and then the process of writing itself began to create more ideas. The ideas flowed more freely and creating content became much easier for me to do.

Today, I've written nine books. If you had asked me five years ago if that was possible, I would have laughed! But the ideas are there. You just have to start capturing them.

One of my clients, Naomi, also didn't know where to start or what to create. So, we simply got started. After she wrote her first blog, she got a roadshow for speaking at five events around the country. As you can see, action really does precede clarity!

Overcoming This Barrier

To overcome this barrier, you just need to get started creating, the way Naomi did. Spend five or 10 minutes every morning writing down ideas for content. More importantly, have a notebook or a spreadsheet open all the time, and every time an idea or notion comes to you, jot it down quickly before you forget. You may think you'll remember, but at the end of the day, with so much more going on in your practice, you likely won't.

Barrier 7: What If I Say the Wrong Thing and Upset Someone?

How often do we say things or do things in the normal course of our week that other people may not like or agree with? Content creation is about showing up and taking the lead on a topic. And we know that leadership often means doing things that feel uncomfortable. I love this quote from Martin Luther King Jr., 'A genuine leader is not a searcher for consensus but a molder of consensus.'

What if people disagree? That's great news. If we all had the same thing to say in life, it would be boring.

The reality is, you don't get anyone to agree with you if you stay silent. It doesn't mean you have to be disagreeable. By sharing your ideas, you help your audience to gain a greater sense of self. Whether they agree or disagree, they get more insights and understanding. As the famous adage says, 'It's the mark of an educated mind to be able to entertain a thought without accepting it.'

I often think of the book *Above the Line* by Michael Henderson[7], culture expert for the New Zealand All Blacks. At a keynote I once heard Michael say, 'If you want to get a greater sense of who you are, have lunch with somebody you don't like.' It's the same thing for your audience. Giving people a greater sense of themselves is one of the greatest gifts you can give. It means there is a higher purpose to your content, and you're giving your audience more insights.

The more you can get clear on who you are and who you're not, the better leader you'll become and the more cut through you'll have. Russell Brunson, in his book *Expert Secrets*, talks about polarising experts.[8] He writes, 'Those who are at the extremes of polarisation will actually have higher levels of people who don't like them or don't agree with them, but those who are in the middle actually are the ones who are least able to connect with people.'[9]

Overcoming This Barrier

To overcome this barrier, remember that you're not here to be vanilla and accommodating (and forgettable). Push the edges a little if you can. People will disagree. And when they do, try not to take it personally and always thank them for their opinion. After all, that's all it is – an opinion.

Barrier 8: I Need to Be Perfect

One of the most common things that holds people back is the idea that they need to be perfect. People compare their initial drawing, note or scribbled thought to a

---

7   Henderson, M. (2014). Above the Line: How to Create a Company Culture that Engages Employees, Delights Customers and Delivers Results. Wiley.

8   Brunson, R. (2017). Expert Secrets: The Underground Playbook to Find Your Message, Build a Tribe, and Change the World. Morgan James Publishing.

9   Brunson. (2017).

published book or blog, and believe that what they've created should be of the same standard.

There is no such thing as perfect. And there is no such thing as *immediately* creating something perfect.

This was a big lesson for me as I started my own consulting practice, and it is for many of my clients as well. When we look at a published author, we can trick ourselves into thinking this incredible genius must have sat down and immediately created a masterpiece, with no need to edit, spellcheck or proofread. It simply popped into their head and onto paper in perfect form.

Many of the clients I speak to don't realise that an author's ideas were initially scrawls or scribbles on a piece of paper, just like theirs. The writer then went through the process of unpacking their mess of thoughts. They researched, wrote drafts, had their work copy-edited, proofread and typeset. There is a process from capturing an idea to distributing it – the content doesn't just magically appear. Who would have thought!?

Overcoming This Barrier

As Margaret Atwood, author of *The Handmaid's Tale*, said, 'If I waited for perfection, I would never write a word.' Just like with many of our barriers, the secret then is just to get started. Put content out, even if it isn't quite perfect. Done is better than perfect – every time.

Barrier 9: Why Would Anyone Hire Me?

Sometimes people play it safe by undervaluing themselves and their ideas. Many of my clients, and women in consulting generally, struggle under the thought, 'Why would someone hire me to do this work? They can easily do it themselves'. Or, 'Why would they pay me for this? My services aren't worth very much.'

This kind of thinking will incapacitate you. You'll find yourself holding back and waiting for someone else to take action (rather than taking action yourself). And it will hold you back from having the confidence you need to build and grow your practice.

Overcoming This Barrier

At the end of the day, only you offer your unique value. There is no one else doing exactly what you do because no one else is you. As long as you are offering a solution to your clients, then they will hire you. Overcoming this barrier means overcoming your mindset. Understanding your own value may take time, but practice living it first.

Be confident when approaching potential clients, or when they approach you. And have a whitepaper available, highlighting your capabilities and offerings. Having this in hand will give you a boost of confidence and get you over that initial hurdle of seeing your own worth.

Barrier 10: I Don't Know What to Charge

Many women in consulting struggle to set good pricing for their consulting services. In fact, I'd say this is one of the biggest challenges to building a consulting practice. It's not always easy to find the pricing that allows us to get paid for our knowledge, insight and services but is also reasonable to our clients.

Most of the women that I work with consistently undervalue the worth of their services and offerings (which also relates to Barrier 9 above). But when you are able to quantify your value, then you build up your own ability to embrace your worth and your right to fair compensation. This is a win-win for both the consultant and the client, as the client who sees that *you* value your work is much more likely to value it as well. But not understanding these can limit your ability to successfully sell yourself and your services.

Overcoming This Barrier

Correct pricing can optimise your revenue from sales and help you to build up your practice. And to get correct pricing you need good benchmarking. Benchmarking delivers potentially powerful insights that can lead to performance and practice improvements. Begin by understanding your pricing and position and that of your competitors. Then see where you stand out or differentiate and analyse how that shifts your placement in the industry. And if you continue to struggle, reach out to an expert for help.

Barrier 11: I Don't Understand My Customer

Many women in consulting fail to adequately understand their customers in the beginning of their consulting journey. But understanding your customer – and their problems – will help you to create offerings that solve those problems for them. Even better, when you understand your customer and their problems, you're in an excellent position to sell to them in an organic or natural way.

Instead of offering them something that you know will help them, you will just feel more pressure about what to offer them. And that makes it hard to sell and hard to build up your practice.

Overcoming This Barrier

To begin to understand your customer you need to talk to them. Reach out to those you think fall within your ideal client demographic and find out what's going on with them. What are their problems? What areas are they struggling with? Asking questions and having conversations is the key to understanding your customer, and creating the solutions that they need.

Barrier 12: I'm Too Busy to Grow

When you're too busy working in your business, you don't have the capacity to work on your business and grow your business. Much of this comes from not managing your boundaries. And, when you don't manage your boundaries well, you can suffer from scope creep.

With scope creep your projects can begin to grow out of control and you lose the ability to sell well. You might feel pressure to maximise each of your sales and to offer more and more value for your client. But rather than leading to an increase in revenue, it actually makes the purchase process more bespoke and more difficult.

This leads to delays in the decision making process and in making more sales. And that leads to an inability to spend the time working on and growing your practice.

Overcoming This Barrier

Be vigilant about managing your boundaries so that you are able to grow your business. You may need to say no more often (something that can be difficult when you want to please your clients), but if you explain why – that you're sticking with the scope of the project, or within your realm of expertise – they will understand. And once you hold your boundaries, you'll be in a great position to help more clients, grow your practice and become a woman with influence in your community.

Key Questions

1. Which of the above barriers holds you back from growing your consulting practice? Is it one or more, or all of them?
2. Why does this or these hold you back?
3. What is the impact of this holding you back? Money? Revenue? Cashflow? Time? Influence?
4. What advice would you give someone else struggling to overcome this barrier?
5. Is the belief you have around this barrier actually true? What would be a more helpful belief to adopt?
6. Based on what you've learned in this chapter, what will you do to overcome that which holds you back?
7. How will you implement this?
8. Who can you ask for advice on overcoming this block?
9. What strategies will you implement to make this sustainable for you?
10. How will you celebrate?

CHAPTER 3

THE FOUR DERAILERS OF YOUR CONSULTING PRACTICE

'The most common way people give up their power is thinking that they don't have any.'

– Alice Walker

Once you've gotten past the barriers to beginning or growing your consulting practice, you might think it will be clear sailing from here on out. This may be the case. But you also need to be aware of some derailers that might come up for you as you move along the trajectory of your practice.

As I mentioned in the previous chapter, in 2008, I started my life again when my husband and I divorced and I left town. What I didn't mention yet is that around the same time, the global financial crisis (or GFC) also occurred. And, to add to my upheaval and sense of loss, I found that I couldn't get a job no matter how many I applied for. I kept applying and failing to get through.

In my personal life, and in my career, these things were massive derailers. They threw me off my personal trajectory, and absolutely nothing seemed to be going right. I'd left my marriage, my home, my town, my career. I'd moved home to my parent's house and I was struggling to find anyone to hire me. I was drowning in the challenges and feeling like there was no way out.

Derailers like this can occur anytime – in our lives and in our work. And they can be anything that throws you off your course. But when you have a consulting practice, there are four derailers that come up more often than others. These are those things that hold people back from really stepping into their personal power and being the consultant that they have the potential to be.

The Four Derailers to Your Consulting Practice

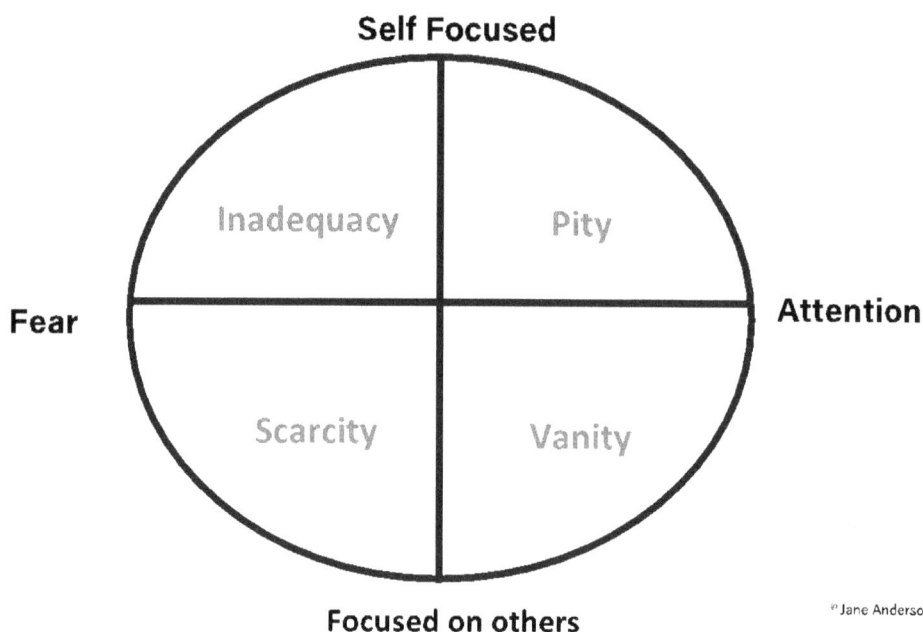

Self Focused

Inadequacy

Pity

Fear

Attention

Scarcity

Vanity

Focused on others

© Jane Anderson

Derailer 1: Inadequacy

Have you ever had the feeling you're not good enough? Not smart enough? Maybe you don't have the degree or the experience. Or maybe you don't have a huge social media following or an extensive email list. Whatever the cause, this sense of inadequacy is sometimes called the 'imposter syndrome'.

We talked about imposter syndrome in the previous chapter. But it's such a widespread and insidious challenge to any business and practice, that it's important to be aware that it can rear its head at any time.

So, what is imposter syndrome?

The imposter syndrome is the name for the fear that someone is going to find you out. That someone is going to look around and realise that you don't belong, or that you don't deserve to be there. That you truly are inadequate.

The imposter syndrome is such a common feeling that it's impacted nearly all of us at some point – or many points – in our careers. Even the most accomplished, well-respected and admired people in the world have struggled with imposter syndrome. This includes celebrities like Sophia Amoruso, Tom Hanks, Sheryl Sandberg, Lady Gaga and Tina Fey.[1] Even Seth Godin has struggled with it during his career.[2]

So if you're feeling this, you're not alone. But if you're not careful, if you allow imposter syndrome to take control, it can most definitely derail all the hard work and growth you've built into your consulting practice.

Overcoming Inadequacy

If you're facing feelings of inadequacy and struggling with imposter syndrome, your next step is to answer these key questions:

- Have you started to make steps towards your goals?

- Are the fears you have ones that you have created in your own mind?

- Have you spoken to an expert, mentor or coach with experience to advise you?

- Have you actually had a conversation with a decision maker you're wanting to influence? Whether it's for a promotion, a new job or to connect with that ideal client, have you had the conversation with them about what you're trying to do and how you can help them?

If you've already faced a setback in your practice because of imposter syndrome or feelings of inadequacy, don't give up. Remember, when you're facing a setback that

---

1 '10 famous people who deal with Imposter Syndrome'. Kajabi. Accessed at https://kajabi.com/blog/celebrities-with-imposter-syndrome.

2 Godin, S. (29 October 2017). 'Imposter Syndrome'. Seth's Blog. Accessed at https://seths.blog/2017/10/imposter-syndrome/.

feels impossible to overcome, it is possible. Many others have been there before you and went on to have incredible practices and careers. Lean into your internal resilience, take a chance and keep moving forward.[3]

Derailer 2: Scarcity

One of the greatest challenges when trying to step out into your space in your practice is fighting the feeling of scarcity.

Scarcity, in terms of economics, is where 'the demand for a good or service is greater than the availability of the good or service'.[4] Scarcity can refer to any number of things. It could be money when you're looking to save for a home. It could be time when you're trying to balance your work and family life. It could be food when you're working on getting fit. But in terms of your consulting practice, scarcity is the notion that there are not enough clients, or not enough work, for you and the rest of your competitors.

Research shows that anytime there is scarcity, there is fixation.[5] So, when people suffer from feelings of scarcity, they fixate on the thing that is scarce – money, food, time or clients.

This is demonstrated in the book, *Scarcity: Why Having Too Little Means So Much*, where the authors share the conclusions from a WWII-era experiment.[6] While the methods are tremendously outdated, the information is telling. In this study, researchers at the University of Minnesota starved healthy subjects, and then experimented with introducing different feeding protocols.

---

3   Buckingham, V. (24 April 2020). 'How to Recover When Your Career Gets Derailed'. Harvard Business Review. Accessed at https://hbr.org/2020/04/how-to-recover-when-your-career-gets-derailed.
4   Scarcity. In National Geographic, Resource Library. Retrieved from National Geographic encyclopedic online database. Accessed at https://www.nationalgeographic.org/encyclopedia/scarcity/#:~:text=Scarcity%20is%20one%20of%20the,ultimately%20make%20up%20the%20economy.
5   Novotney, A. (February 2014). 'The psychology of scarcity'. American Psychological Association. Accessed at https://www.apa.org/monitor/2014/02/scarcity.
6   Mullainathan, S. and Shafir, E. (2013). Scarcity: Why Having Too Little Means So Much. Times Books.

What they discovered was that each of the subjects became obsessed with food. They traded information about food, read recipe books and even fantasised about opening cafes and restaurants.[7] And even when they had enough food, they still saw the world through the perspective of food scarcity.

This holds true when we feel there is a scarcity of clients or work in our practices. And it has the same outcomes. When you're looking at the world from a place of scarcity, you'll find yourself distracted by what everyone else is doing. Your mental bandwidth is all taken up with focusing on what you lack – rather than focusing on what you could be doing to grow and further your own practice. You spend all your time worrying that all the opportunities have gone, all the jobs are taken or that no one has the money or can afford to hire you. And that leaves no time for anything else.

Overcoming Scarcity

In order to overcome feelings of scarcity, you need to see whether or not your assumptions are actually true. Are the jobs really all taken? Have the opportunities honestly all gone? Pick up the phone and ask the right people the right questions to find the answers. More often than not, these assumptions simply aren't true. The jobs and opportunities are still there.

So what then is causing these feelings of scarcity? Fear, most likely. But understanding where these feelings come from and knowing the truth (that there's work enough for you) is the first step. Then you need to put your blinkers on and stop comparing yourself to others.

Derailer 3: Pity

When things don't go the way you want or expect it can be very frustrating. And sometimes this is just the way life (and work goes). It can seem like no matter what you do, nothing works. And when these things happen, you might begin questioning why this is happening to you or what you've done wrong.

---

7   Mullainathan (2013).

So then you might tell your partner or your friend and colleague about what is going on. And it's likely they'll feel sorry for you. This validates how you're already feeling. Maybe you even start to enjoy the pity, which can cause you to wallow in it even more.

In every practice, things do go wrong at times. And we all feel sorry for ourselves once in a while. But wallowing in this emotion is one of the biggest derailers you could face in your practice.

When we're in the midst of self-pity it's really difficult to take a step back and gain some perspective about how to fix the challenge that we're facing. Because of that we can get 'stuck' in the problem, unable to rouse ourselves enough to brainstorm a solution to the situation. The 'poor me' mentality isolates us and limits our capacity to move forward into a better place in our practice.

Overcoming Pity

If this is you, there are a few steps to take. First, put a deadline on the emotion. Allow yourself to feel the emotions, but recognise that they're not going to get you anywhere. Then swap self-pity for self-compassion. Remind yourself that things can go wrong for anyone and recognise that you're not alone. Zoom out with your perspective and try to see the bigger picture. Sure one thing went wrong – that could happen to anyone. But look at all the things that are going well.

Now, take control by brainstorming real solutions to your challenges. Then take some action based on those potential solutions. In fact, taking action is a powerful way to change how you feel.[8] And if you're struggling to step out of the situation on your own, ask for real help from someone you trust. When you're able to stop being at the mercy of your circumstances or playing the victim, and can take action to make a change to your circumstance, you'll be able to move past pity and back into progress.

---

8   Kanter, R. (28 March 2011). 'Four Reasons Any Action Is Better than None'. Harvard Business Review. Accessed at https://hbr.org/2011/03/four-reasons-any-action-is-bet.html.

Derailer 4: Vanity

Seeking validation is only natural when gaining a sense of identity. However, when you get that validation for putting out only what's 'popular', you aren't necessarily being your most powerful you. More importantly, your focus is on yourself, rather than on your clients.

One example of this is, of course, vanity metrics. Vanity metrics are data points that appear impressive to other people but don't give you any insight about where you are now and where your practice should move in the future. They are also easy to manipulate and can make you and others believe you are successful without driving any meaningful results (like growth in clients or revenue).

Do you constantly seek likes and comments on your social media feed? Do you need to be reassured all the time? When people aren't liking or commenting on your posts or articles, do you take it personally and feel affronted or worried that you've somehow lost? Vanity metrics – likes, comments, followers, page views, etc. – are named 'vanity' metrics for a very important reason. They simply don't matter other than to 'look good'.

Outside of vanity metrics, the drive to feel popular can derail your practice. If someone unsubscribes from your mailing list, this is information that can drive your future email marketing strategies in the future. When someone disagrees with a position you've taken in your content, you now have a better understanding of who your clients are. But when you allow vanity to rear its head, instead of taking this information and creating better strategies for your practice, you might allow it to derail you.

This is not stepping into your power. This is playing the popularity contest. And it will keep you as a follower not a leader.

Overcoming Vanity

Stop measuring vanity metrics, and look instead at engagement metrics. On social media, for example, who is engaging with you regularly? When you send an EDM, who takes up your offers or congratulates you on your success? Who is reaching out to you via your website? Is your business growing? Are you selling your programs and helping your clients? These are the metrics that you need to track and measure. And these are the metrics that will help you grow your practice into a thriving consulting business.

Takeaway

When I was derailed from my marriage, my home, my town, my job and my life, I was tremendously disempowered. Things were happening to me where I didn't feel like I had any choices and I felt completely out of control. Still, I didn't just sit back and become a victim of my circumstances. I took action. I shook off the self-pity, stopped worrying about what anyone would think about me and recognised that even though there was some scarcity (jobs were hard to come by during the GFC), there was still enough to go around.

I began to concentrate on figuring out what kind of company or role resonated as my dream job. I knew there was someone out there who needed my help. I just needed to find them. So, I set out to find that 'someone' and approached a company that met those criteria. They had a need for the help I could provide, and they were the kind of company I'd always dreamed of working for. They hired me and it was an excellent fit for both of us.

Inadequacy, scarcity, pity and vanity – these can be heavy derailers to your ability to become a 'woman with influence' and grow your practice. They aren't unusual. Many of the incredible women featured in this book have had to overcome the same derailers. But they have done so and they have had amazing success since then. And you can as well.

Once you are aware of these derailers, you can take active steps to avoid their impact in your work life.

🔑 Key questions

1. What are you most afraid of, really?
2. Which quadrant most resonates for you in your practice?
3. When was a time when you felt derailed in the past?
4. What caused it?
5. How did you solve it?
6. What would you do if you had your time again?
7. If you were to advise someone who may be experiencing the same challenges and fears as you about how to avoid these derailers, what advice would you give them?

CHAPTER 4

WHAT MAKES A SUCCESSFUL CONSULTING PRACTICE

'I never dreamed about success, I worked for it.'

– Estee Lauder

Growing a consulting practice is possibly one of the toughest things you'll ever do in your life. You are on your own with no team, no marketing department, no IT department and no reception.

You're it.

And when you're just watching others from afar, they can make it seem so easy. These established coaches write their blogs, share motivational memes and quotes on Instagram, post the exotic locations and hotels they're staying in and the private drivers that pick them up from the airport. They make it look so prestigious and amazing, and even easy.

The truth is that this hasn't happened overnight for those women either. They have put in late nights and early mornings to be able to get their practice to where it is right now, and where they need and want it to be. And they have the motivation and drive to make it work.

There is no plan B.

Those who make it look easy are typically doing three things that are working really well for them. First, they know how to market. Second, they know how to sell. And third, they have great systems in place to be able to play in their genius zone.

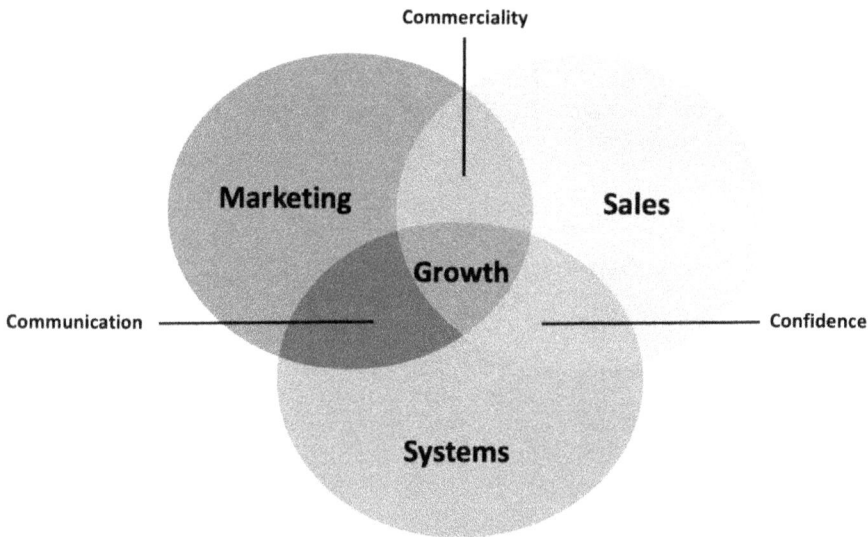

© Jane Anderson

Marketing

Being able to market your consulting practice is often the biggest challenge a corporate consultant will face. But if you are having sales issues then it's usually because of a marketing and positioning problem.

Whilst the concept of marketing and how it leads into the customer sales experience hasn't changed too much, the mechanics of how it works have. According to McKinsey, 10 years ago the average consumer who was looking to purchase a vehicle would visit five sales yards. Today, the data tells us this number is now less than two. So a lot more information is now online and a lot more research can be done than ever before.

Consumers are making decisions about you, your services and how you can help them without you even knowing it. Let's have a look at the four key areas to consider when marketing your practice.

```
                        Know Someone
                             │
                             │
        Educate              │         Direct Contact
                             │
                             │
 ┌──────────────┐            │                    ┌──────────────┐
 │  Don't Know  │────────────┼────────────────────│  Know What   │
 │  What I Want │            │                    │   I Want     │
 └──────────────┘            │                    └──────────────┘
                             │
        Awareness            │      Network or Search
                             │
                             │
                     Don't Know Someone
```

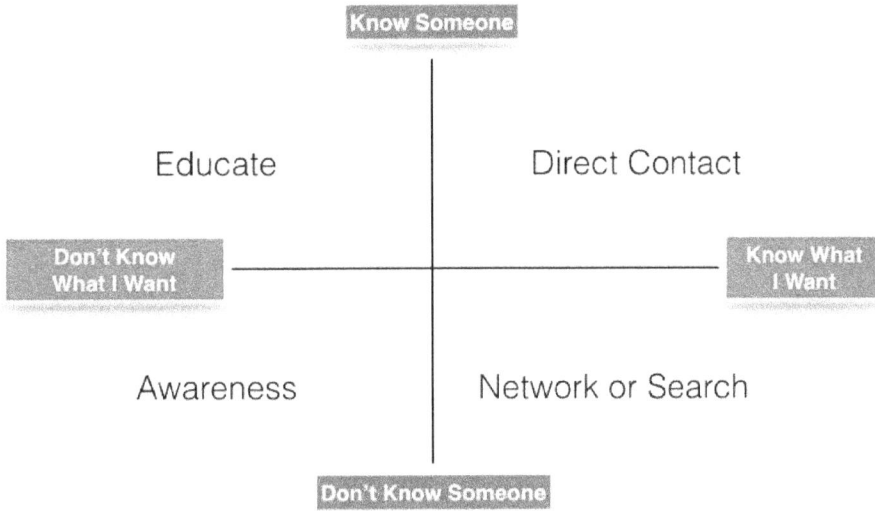

©Jane Anderson

Direct Contact

'I know someone who can help me and I know what I want.'

In the past, customers sought the services of people they remembered. They knew what they wanted and they knew who could help them. From a business perspective, you also knew your customers and understood their needs. You might have had a customer database, even if it was a simple file of cards! Direct contact was a highly effective way of doing business.

When I managed a retail shoe store, I kept a list of customers with details on their shoe size and the brands they loved. I fondly remember a customer called Mrs Thomas, who always bought size nine shoes and loved a brand called Lorbac. They were beautiful shoes and always fitted her perfectly.

A pair of Lorbac shoes cost about $300, and each season I would set aside every size nine pair of Lorbac shoes that came in and called Mrs Thomas. She always bought them all! And throughout the year, whenever Mrs Thomas needed a new pair of shoes, she knew she could call me to see if I had anything that would suit her. I knew her and she knew me. Sometimes, I would even see things in other stores she might like and let her know about them.

I didn't receive any commission on sales, but it helped that I knew her likes and dislikes. She trusted my taste and I didn't waste her time.

Network or Search

'I don't know someone who can help me, but I know what I want.'

In the past, if a customer needed help with something but didn't know who to turn to, they would either ask their network – usually family and friends – for recommendations, or open the phone book and do a search.

The advice from family and friends was based on brand recall from magazine, television and radio advertising. This meant that trying to remain top of mind was an expensive exercise.

In terms of search, businesses needed to be as close to the top of the listings in the phone book as possible. Many businesses opted for names that started with 'A' – for example, Aardvark Consulting – so customers were more likely to see them first. This was the equivalent of today's organic Google search. Think of paying for a big ad in the phone book like investing in Google AdWords today.

Awareness

'I don't know someone who can help me and I don't know what I want.'

In a pre-digital world, to get in front of the people you didn't know and who didn't know you, you had to invest in media advertising, billboards, public relation campaigns and cold calling. Creating awareness was a lengthy, expensive process.

Public speaking was also part of this process and there was a heavy emphasis on getting in front of new clients. US marketing guru Seth Godin really pioneered public speaking for business with his books *Permission Marketing*[1] and *Tribes*[2].

Today we have much higher return on activities where people already know us, such as working with our databases.

Educate

'I know who can help me but I don't know what I want.'

This quadrant represents the greatest shift in the customer journey. In the pre-digital world, businesses had mailing lists – but the way they educated the people on these lists was with print material, such as newsletters, flyers and catalogues. The problem was, these were rarely educational or interesting. Newsletters were also often done half-heartedly and irregularly. They failed to effectively target and educate those people who were aware of the business, but didn't realise they had a problem that needed solving.

Sales

Most women consultants I work with would rather do anything but sell. But the good news is that it can be a lot more fun and enjoyable if you've got a plan, an approach and a strategy.

There are three key timeframes to take into account when you are selling consulting programs. These are:

1. before selling
2. during the sales meeting
3. after the sales meeting

---

1   Godin, S. (1999). Permission Marketing: Turning Strangers Into Friends And Friends Into Customers. Simon & Schuster.
2   Godin, S. (2011). Tribes: We need you to lead us. Piatkus.

	BEFORE	**DURING**	**AFTER**
WE	③ Content **POSITIONING** Unprepared	⑥ Next Steps **DECISION** Drag	⑨ Value **SUCCESS** Once-off
YOU	② Challenges **EMPATHY** Pressure	⑤ Understanding **INSIGHT** Trust	⑧ Relationships **INFLUENCE** Traction
ME	① Clarity **IDENTITY** Hard to buy	④ Leadership **PRESENCE** Assumptions	⑦ Resources **CONTRACT** Cashflow

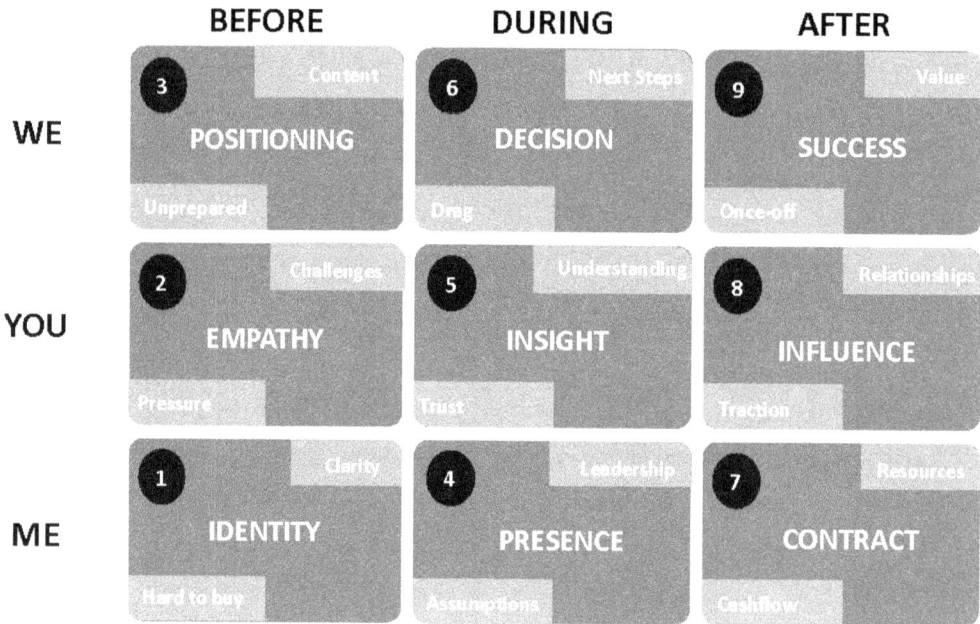

© Jane Anderson

BEFORE

Before the sales meeting there are three key areas to consider:

- **Identity:** The first is looking at yourself and who you are. You need to have a strong sense of clarity about what you bring to the table, the programs that you're selling, how much they cost and how they're delivered, before you engage in any active selling or sales meeting. You don't have to have designed the whole program or written all the material. But you need to at least know what will be in the program and how you're going to deliver it when the time comes. If you don't have this clarity you're going to be very hard to buy from.

- **Empathy:** The second is empathy and connection with the customer. Empathy and connection allow you to understand the challenges and experiences of your clients and customers. And this helps you to create programs and offerings that focus on solving their problems. If you can't tap into the specific problems and challenges that they're experiencing, or that they would say they are experiencing, the customer will feel that you don't really understand them. And they may feel pressured into buying. This situation is uncomfortable for both the buyer and seller. So to find ease and enjoyment in the selling process, we need to take the time to really understand what's happening with them.

- **Positioning:** The third is positioning. You need to create the framing so that when you go into a sales meeting the customer has a very clear understanding about who you are and what you do. This means being able to create really powerful, cut-through collateral that can create this framing and ensure that you're addressing the customer's problems. You never want to go into a sales meeting empty handed. The right piece of collateral can help your customer understand your value long before you walk in the door. If you don't have any collateral, you will come across as unprepared and you'll spend the entire time trying to catch the client up on your value, as opposed to being focused on solving their problem for them (and potentially making a sale!).

DURING

During the sales meeting there are three other key areas to really focus on:

- **Presence:** The first is your own presence. You need to come into the meeting being totally present with the customer. You can do this when you've prepared excellent collateral that you know you can rely on to sell your program. This allows you to just sit and focus on exactly what the customer is saying and be comfortable and relaxed. You don't have to worry about conveying your 'value' or the background of your offering – it's all in your collateral. Instead, you can focus on the client, asking the strong questions to really clarify what is happening for them.

When you're focusing on the customer, they feel safe and they trust you. If you don't, they will feel short-changed as they listen to you 'sell' rather than try to 'solve' their problems. During the sales meeting you also need to be prepared to walk away if the fit isn't right, or you don't have the right response to the customer's problem.

- **Insight:** Insight is ensuring that you have a way to define exactly where your customer is in their journey. You also need to be able to help the customer see for themselves where they are in that journey. That means coming into every sales meeting with really powerful sense-making skills so you can translate the customer's experiences and 'symptoms' to diagnose their real issue. Only in that way will you know how to solve those issues for them or, importantly, demonstrate to the customer why you are proposing the solutions you are proposing.

  Without that translation, your customers will lose trust in you. They'll feel like they're just being sold something (anything!) as opposed to you genuinely having thought about and translated those problems into a solution.

- **Decision:** During the meeting you can expect one of three possible decisions. The first is 'Yes, we want to go ahead.' The second is 'No, we don't want to go ahead.' The third is 'We're not sure. We need to think about it or talk to other people.' It's important to remember that any of those three decisions are a good outcome because you're walking out of the meeting knowing exactly what the next step is.

  If the decision is yes, then your next step is to determine the dates to proceed. If the decision is no, then the next step is to simply thank them for their time and move on. If the decision is that they need to think about it or talk to more people, then your next step is to schedule the follow up. Will you meet again in two weeks, or call in a week? In this case, you also need to find out what else they might need from you or who else you might need to meet with in order to get a decision.

  The one thing that you don't want to do is walk out of the meeting not knowing what the next steps are. If you do this, then your program will certainly drag on and you won't get any decisions at all.

AFTER

After the sales meeting there are three elements as well:

- **Contract:** If the client says yes to your program, then you're going to have to ensure that you have everything you need to deliver that program. This includes your team, contractors if you're engaging and using them, your internal resources, etc. To do this well, you must have a solid contract in place. If you don't then you won't get paid in a timely fashion and you'll be open to cash flow problems. You might also suffer from project and time creep which can roll out for a long time.

  I had a program that was designed to be delivered over a nine-month period. However, it took four years to complete that program because of the level of complex change that was going on. So it's important to be mindful of milestones. You should also consider progress payments and indicators of when they need to be paid.

- **Influence:** Influence means knowing and understanding which people you most need to build a relationship with in the organisation in order to ensure the success of the program. You cannot depend on just one person or the person signing the cheque. You need to know who the players are in the organisation who have the greatest influence over the success of the program.

  Engage with them and you'll get the greatest result. Fail to do so and your program will struggle to gain traction because the right people have not been taken on the journey to understand the value you're delivering.

- **Success:** Work to extrapolate your success across the entire organisation. You can do this by continuing to sell the program within the organisation itself, whether that's delivering it again in subsequent years, or delivering it to a new team or department. This works particularly well if you have a program that is designed for teams across a whole organisation, for example, productivity or resilience.

However, to do this you need to be able to measure the value and progress within the program so that you can show the decision maker the return on investment for the organisation. Understanding their return on investment helps the organisation feel like they're having success.

But it's not just a matter of measuring it at the end of the program's delivery. You need to continually measure through the process so they're seeing results and tangible outcomes along the way. If you aren't able to do this you'll end up as a one-program wonder.

Systems

Having a practice and being able to market and sell within that practice is crucial. If you can't sell you simply won't have a practice. However, once you start selling you'll start to get busy. Then you're off and juggling a lot of programs, a lot of people and a lot of logistics.

Once you're about two years into your practice you'll likely start to see some glaring holes in your systems. Gaps like having checklists for projects and tasks start to emerge simply because you're struggling to hold too much in your head. You're needing to organise some support but, when everything is in your head, it can feel like it's just easier to do it yourself.

One of the biggest challenges I find when working with women who are building their consulting practices is that they are used to doing everything. They can also struggle to find help. The good news, however, is that there are lots of people out there who are very willing to help and support you and give you what you need to build and grow your systems and your practice. And once you are able to delegate, you'll find you will sleep much better at night.

There are three key areas for you to elevate your systems, grow your practice and create scale. These are clarity, visibility and accountability.

FLOW

Clarity   **Visibility**

COHESION

FOCUSED ———————   ————————— FINISHED

Accountability

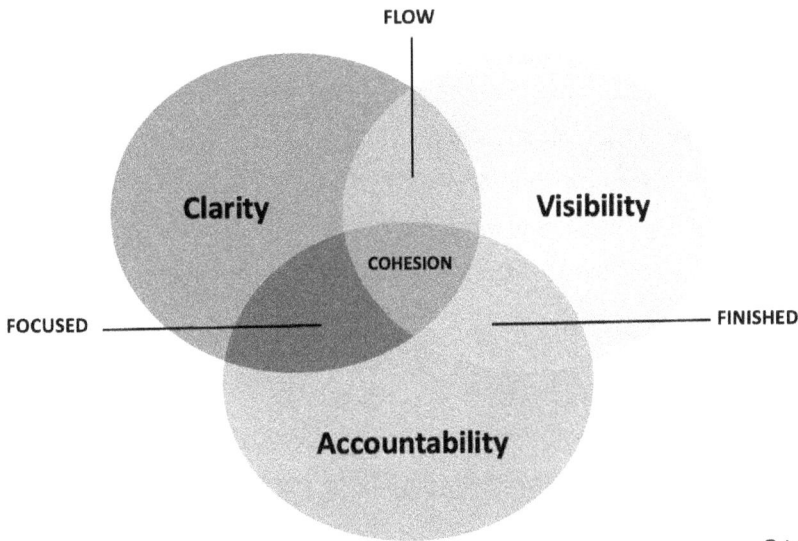

© Jane Anderson

1. **Clarity:** Clarity in your systems is about being clear on the programs that you run, the projects that you need to deliver and the systems that you need in place to allow you to succeed. This includes the habits and routines that you need in your practice every day, week, month, quarter and year. For example, every day you will need one of your team members to help you to check your LinkedIn messages and your sales pipeline and follow up on anyone who is outstanding. Every week you will need someone to help you with your bookkeeping or invoicing. And every month you will need someone to help you create content or socials, for example.

   You also need clarity about the specific tasks and how to do those tasks so your team understands precisely what you need from them. In fact, 50% of people don't understand what's expected of them at work.[3] You don't want

---

3   Rigoni, B. and Nelson, B. (27 September 2016). 'Do Employees Really Know What's Expected of Them?' Gallup. Accessed at https://www.global-integration.com/insights/half-of-people-dont-know-what-is-expected-of-them-at-work/#:~:text=A%20recent%20Gallup%20survey%20on,were%20equally%20unclear%20about%20expectations.

to be in this statistic, so the more efficient systems you have in place, the more clarity you can create.

2. **Visibility:** One of the biggest challenges with employees is having visibility of their work. They may have calendars but they may also just be using a piece of paper and a pen for their task list. The disconnect that happens between those two things is a major problem and a huge gap in systems, particularly for consultants who are in the growth stage.

   The purpose of a calendar is to allow you to see your employees' capacity and exactly what it is that they have on their plate. But if you don't also have their task lists, then you don't have full visibility of all the work on those lists. This means that you aren't able to manage them as well as you should. But it also means that there's a major black hole where tasks and projects are at risk of getting lost.

3. **Accountability:** We all need deadlines to know what is expected and when, so that the work can get done. We can't just say, 'Oh at some point that will get done' and hope for the best. We need accountability of tasks – who is responsible for them and when they are due. If these two questions aren't answered, people will feel lost or frustrated and then they may start to blame each other or even you.

   On the other hand, where there is appropriate and transparent allocation of the work, with a set timeframe for completion, people are able to complete their work and understand their own accountability. One of the biggest mistakes we make as experts is to try to get everything done right now by managing everything ourselves. But this doesn't allow for our employees and contractors to be accountable for themselves. They need to know how to plan their own work around their own capacity and time so that we can hold them accountable but, first and foremost, they can hold themselves accountable. This will allow you to work better together.

If you can get the clarity and visibility right, what happens is that workflows move and get momentum instead of staying stagnant and stuck in quicksand. If you can get the visibility and accountability working right, your work will get finished, and tasks and projects will get completed. You will also have a sense of accomplishment because you've achieved something. If you can get clarity and accountability working right, your energy and resources are focused on getting the right support aligned with priorities, and what needs to get done, gets done in the timeframes required.

If you can get these three key areas working in terms of your systems, you're going to get much better support and ultimately be able to scale your practice.

🔑 Key Questions

1. What programs will you be selling and delivering to your clients?
2. Where will you be delivering and marketing them?
3. How much will you charge?
4. How will you be marketing them?
5. How often do you attend sales meetings empty-handed?
6. How much time is writing proposals costing you?
7. How present are you in your sales meetings?
8. How are you measuring the impact and success of your programs?
9. What systems do you have to scale your practice?
10. Do you have your systems set up to help you deliver your projects, as well as the daily, weekly, monthly, quarterly and annual tasks you need to deliver?

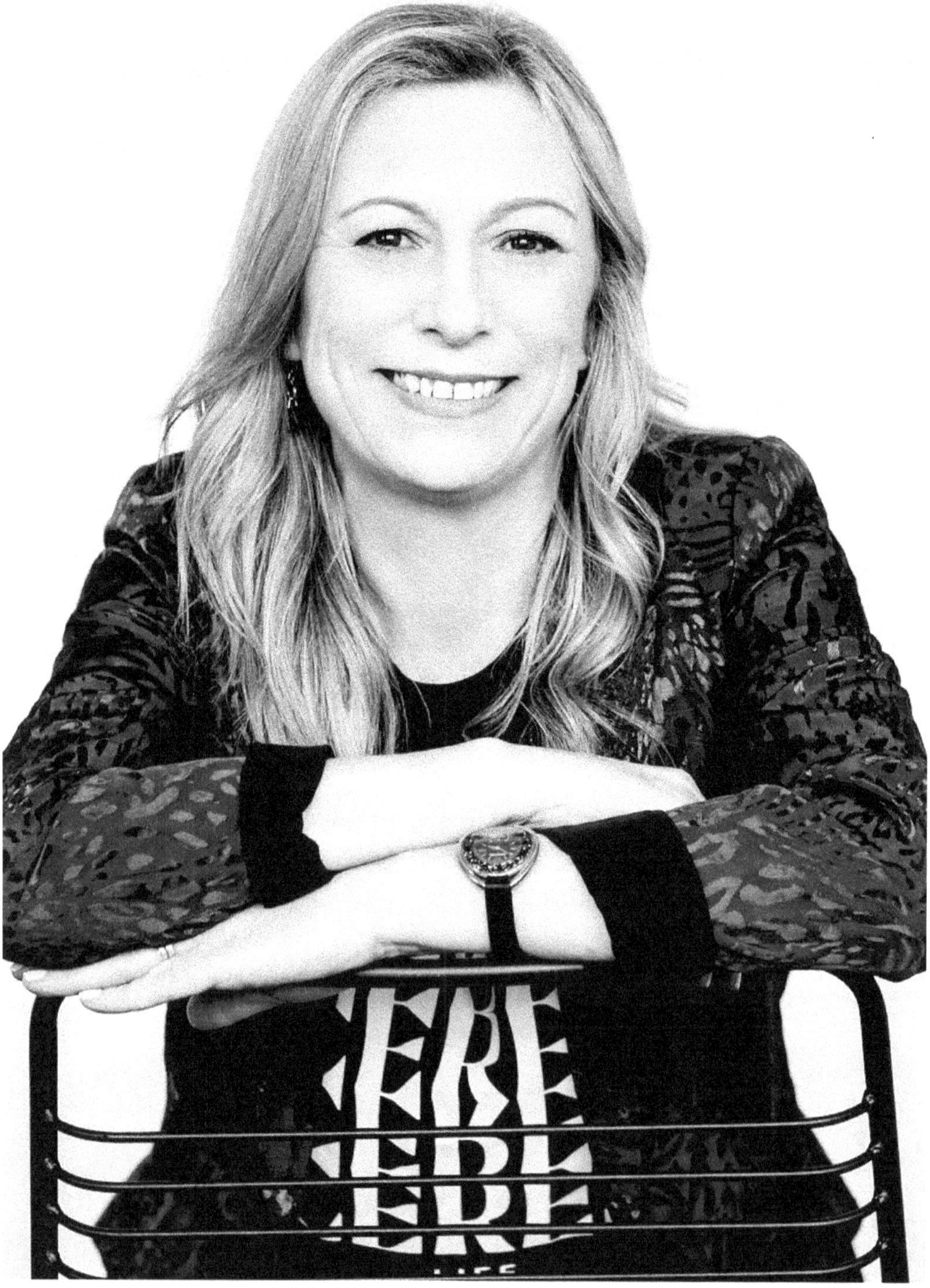

CHAPTER 5

Alison Crabb

Retail Leadership Expert

ARTICULATING YOUR VALUE

Alison Crabb is more than an advocate for human connection in her practice – she's obsessed with it. She's gone from a corporate background, looking after the largest and most successful division in Flight Centre, to now helping other large organisations, particularly retailers, achieve a similar success. But each step of the way she's been focused on connecting and growing *people*.

25 years at Flight Centre made Alison realise that with only one product to sell (travel) the only asset there really is, is the people. And with a team of 1,400 at one stage, leading 212 stores across five brands, she became an expert at running large teams. For Alison, the number one thing that really drove her results was people development, and particularly leadership development.

'Leadership development was my number one strategy. So it's always been my thing, my passion,' says Alison.

Today, Alison is a retail leadership expert, including author, trainer, mentor, coach and speaker, and runs her own consultancy, Alison Crabb Consulting. But it wasn't 100% smooth sailing to get here. And part of the hard work for her was around articulating her own value. She needed to be able to clearly see why her clients needed her (their challenges and desires), how her services worked best and what she offered that was unique to her. This is where the real work occurred.

When People Are the Point of Difference

At 50 Alison was highly successful in her career at Flight Centre. But she knew it was time for a change and wanted to share the golden IP she had been developing along the way. With some time off, a European holiday and some reflection, she decided it was time to launch her own practice. With a miniscule six-month turnaround, she launched.

The decision to move into her own business was a pretty easy one. Yes, she'd met some amazing revenue goals in her previous career (bringing Flight Centre from $18 million to a $49 million profit). And her many accolades, such as winning Flight Centre's Director's Award for Global Outstanding Achievement and becoming a finalist in the Telstra Business Women's Awards, attest to the results she achieves. But what was more important to her was supporting her central business ethos of 'inspiring the humanity of business'. She knew that her heart and soul lay with developing leaders in humanness and connection.

> *You don't build a business. You build people and people build the business.*

Today, Alison delivers retail leadership programs to some of the best retails brands in Australia. She delivers speaking, training, coaching and consulting services to help area leaders in particular.

One of Alison's favourite quotes is by Zig Ziglar: 'You don't build a business. You build people and people build the business.'[1]

Challenges, Milestones and Pivots

Like many in our community, it wasn't a perfect arc to success for Alison. She found herself facing many challenges, milestones and opportunities to pivot along the way.

---

1   Ziglar, T. 'You don't build a business'. Ziglar. Accessed at https://www.ziglar.com/articles/dont-build-business/.

Certainly, she struggled in the face of COVID-19 upheavals, like most consultants. In fact, she found herself with an empty diary in the course of just a couple of days in early 2020.

However, she wasn't about to sit around and wallow in misery. She decided to make the most of the situation and create a game-changing piece of collateral for her business. This is her book, *The Essential Guide for Area Leaders in Retail*.[2] It gives excellent advice around the key elements of the area leader role, including proven strategies, tools and templates to assist them in fulfilling their roles, becoming more effective and delivering better overall results.

Her book has also given incredible growth to Alison in her practice, as well as to the organisations that she works with now. Alison describes the book as prescriptive – a 'how to' guide describing how to be an impactful area leader or area manager. Even better, it shows leaders how to do it in a way where they don't have to work 20 hours a day. And it finally brought all her niche learning together in one place.

Over lockdown, she suddenly had the time to dedicate to her book. Alison describes it as a firm commitment: "'That's it", I said, "I'm just going to focus on this book." And because it was all in my head and I knew my content, it wasn't a hard book to write. It was just focusing and being disciplined on the time. So I made a commitment that I would, over the next however long it would take, write 500 words a day.'

13 weeks later the book was written and sent off to the editor. Then it went to the designer and, in September 2020, it arrived. But this book was more than just a physical piece of her golden IP and thought leadership. It was also exactly what she needed to finally articulate her value.

Articulating Her Value

For Alison, when writing the book, she was forced to think about what it is she really does. Who does she really help? What problems does she really solve? And who benefits the most from her unique take on the business? She quickly realised that this was in the retail space.

---

2   Crabb, A. (2020). The Essential Guide for Area Leaders in Retail. Alison Crabb Consulting.

So, as the book developed, it became a very specific book for retail. Even more so, it became focused on a very specific role in retail (area management), which, in Alison's eyes, is the best retail job in the world and, when done well, has the greatest impact on results for the retailer.

Writing the book really helped her articulate her own value around how she meets and solves the problems of the large retailers that she worked for. And it also helped her demonstrate her extensive expertise in this space. Before she knew it messages were pouring in.

Alison says, 'I was getting LinkedIn messages and emails from great retailers saying, "I got your book. It's so on point. It's very specific to the role. You clearly know this role. We'd love to have a chat." It was hugely exciting to be able to reach so many driven retailers at once.'

Although *The Essential Guide for Area Leaders in Retail* is a passion piece in Alison's eyes, it was exactly what she needed to carve out her place as an expert in the retail industry. From there on her practice began to evolve.

Niching For Success

Until the book, Alison had often found it difficult to demonstrate her strategies, especially as she would often have only a 20 to 30 minute meeting to articulate her worth. It was particularly taxing in retail where she came up against the entrenched belief from retailers that their own in-house training would cut it. But once she'd written the *The Essential Guide*, she had a physical representation of her value, and the framework for quickly and effectively conveying that to others. More importantly, perhaps, she was really able to elevate her positioning.

Because she was so specific it became really easy for others in the space to talk about her. There hadn't been a book written specifically for retail area managers before and those in the industry began to talk about her to others in similar roles. She was easy to talk about and easy to refer to because it was very clear what she did and who she did it for.

This elevated positioning led her to one of her most important clients to date. Out of the blue she was contacted by a billionaire in Monaco, the key founder of some of Australia's biggest retailers, who had read the book and was keen to work with her. Another major brand had shared her book because after only two days of implementing her Ultimate Area Leader Program, they'd already received incredible feedback. And of course, the successes didn't stop there. Through developing this single piece of collateral she had articulated her value and as a result is now working for some of his biggest brands.

Although it can feel challenging to niche and takes much courage to do so, it means you're so much more referable and can be known as the expert in your particular field.

Alison says, 'The closer I got to saying I'm a retail leadership expert, or I specifically work with area leaders, state managers, executive teams, the more successful I became. It changed everything'. She also states the narrower she became (by focusing on retail) the easier her processes became. 'I know their problems and I know what they need to know. Writing a newsletter or a blog became so much easier. And now I've got the cadence of writing regularly because I know who I'm writing to and what I need to be writing about.'

> *Although it can feel challenging to niche and takes much courage to do so, it means you're so much more referable and can be known as the expert in your particular field.*

Game-Changing Collateral

So she had the book, and she had proof it worked. Alison's next step was to leverage the book and really start to hone and elevate her positioning around retail. Even with clients in other industries, sports, and travel, 70% was retail and she knew it was time to jump in with both feet. But to do this she needed the right collateral to help make the selling process efficient and effective.

Alison joined our Joyful Selling with Influence group. During her work with me she honed in on all of her collaterals to ensure that everything was on point, clear and informative. She needed these items to make sure anybody who received them understood quickly and easily exactly what she did and, more importantly, how she could help them solve their problems.

The biggest piece of collateral, that's made the biggest difference to Alison? Having a brochure. Alison describes a typical meeting prior to having a brochure. She says, 'I would go into an organisation. I'd listen to their challenges. I'd go away. I'd put a proposal together, even though I knew what 80% of their challenges were going to be. I'd send them the proposal. And then I'd spend weeks chasing them up, asking, "How did you find the proposal? Where are we now?" It was a long, drawn-out process.'

The brochure changed everything. Now she presents them with a brochure that articulates very clearly that she knows what the problems are, what the solutions should be and what that work will cost. Alison's brochure essentially conveys, 'This is how I can help you and this is what you'd be looking at'. And the feedback has been terrific. Every retailer that she's met with since putting that brochure into her sales process has been impressed. They believe that she knows her stuff. That she understands their specific problems. And, most importantly, what it will cost to solve those problems.

> **At the end of the day, when you know where your expertise lies and who you serve, your next step is to get all your collaterals in place so you elevate your positioning and streamline the selling process.**

Having your value articulated on paper makes selling really easy, vastly speeding up the selling process. And it works. Alison reports that this selling technique helped her sell a $50,000 program in 40 minutes with a retailer that previously she couldn't even get a meeting with because they typically did all their own in-house training. They got the brochure, they bought the book, they loved the book and they wanted the program. They could see the value without her selling it.

At the end of the day, when you know where your expertise lies and who you serve, your next step is to get all your collaterals in place so you elevate your positioning and streamline the selling process.

Describing Your Value

Alison explains that, when you have this success, you see how important it is to harness the process. In fact, it's vital you ensure that, at each of your customer touchpoints, you're allowing the collateral to do the talking for you. This includes books and brochures, of course, but also LinkedIn profiles and websites.

Having this collateral in place means that you're in an excellent position to articulate your value, even when you're not in the room. In fact, Alison believes that being transparent and up-front about her value (through her collateral) saves her an incredible amount of time which she'd otherwise be wasting on the to and fro that can happen when building client relationships. It also saves her the stress and anxiety that can go hand-in-hand with a drawn-out process.

For Alison, having her value proposition right, and being able to easily convey that to her potential clients, has brought exponential results. By changing her program to a per person price (for example, one of the programs is now set at $3,000 per person rather than as a $70,000 program) it's a very easy decision for retailers to make. They now can see that the costs are $3,000 for a senior leader for a six-month program, and they're able to run the numbers and see whether that's in their budget and the return it could give on their investment.

> *Having her value proposition right, and being able to easily convey that to her potential clients, has brought exponential results.*

Getting the Right Systems in Place

With growth came the need to get the right systems in place. Working together we were able to help her stand out with her systems, ultimately elevating her influence and growing her practice. From list building to connecting on LinkedIn and even to getting to know the best systems for her needs, automating helped make Alison's practice run with less friction and fewer bottlenecks. This freed her up to grow her brand more.

Part of Alison's approach is hiring for people's strengths by outsourcing to experts. Rather than hiring overseas or having one business manager that does everything, she has divided up the tasks to the specialists that she needs in each particular area. And she uses regular catch-ups as well as communication systems such as Asana and Active Campaign to keep everything running like clockwork and her team engaged and efficient. But she hasn't stopped there.

When we launched our new program, Practice in a Box, Alison and the team ran with it and saved over six months of work by systematising everything from coaching clients to her Area Leader Programs.

Alison says, 'I think being part of the Women with Influence community has saved me time and money. I'm not having to try out multiple different systems or tools. Jane is very clear on which systems work best for which practice, depending on where that practice is.' The range of technology available to us is so vast and varied that it's hard to know where to start. Having a community to rely on for those things has been invaluable for Alison.

Moving On

Having these systems in place frees Alison up to move on to her next book. The focus of this one will be more innovative and strategic approaches in retail, designed for implementation by area, regional and general managers. Of course, for Alison, the conversation will still be around people. And this will naturally include how people in retail and retail customers are responding to and innovating around COVID-19.

Retail is really struggling with the knock-on effects of COVID-19. And with a typically younger workforce, challenges due to lockdowns, unhappy customers because of check-in and vaccination requirements, availability of products impacted by supply delays, and wait times blowing out because of staff illness and absenteeism, it's not looking to get any better. And all of this also impacts on employee retention. Alison believes there's never been a more important time than right now to be focusing on people in retail and, in her words, 'looking after them'. I'm excited to see what solutions she comes up with!

🔑 3 Key Learnings

1. Build your list from the start – capture data, connect on LinkedIn, create lead-generating collateral and do this all early so you avoid missing out on important contacts!
2. Invest in your collateral – ensure you're telling the right story at the right time.
3. Get consistent – systematise everything so no one falls through the cracks (and save yourself those 3am awakenings!).

***Listen to the Jane Anderson Show Podcast, Episode 64
– Retail Leadership Expert, Alison Crabb***

CHAPTER 6

Renee Giarrusso

Specialist Leadership and Communications Expert

GETTING THE BASICS RIGHT

Renee Giarrusso has always had a love of learning and growth and a drive to be of service to others ever since she was a small child. And she's also been a poet (and a lover of words) since the tender, sweet age of nine. Now, as an adult, these lifelong passions have come together to drive her to her calling within her work – as a leadership and communications expert.

In her work Renee is obsessed with seeing people reach their full potential, within their business and their lives. So since 2006 she has worked with leaders to successfully maximise their potential and the potential of their people and their teams to help them to really get to that next level and master their cut-through communication.

While the root of her work started as a small child, it was just after university that she got one of her most important lessons. Renee's father, at the early age of 49, passed away the night before her last assessment at her first corporate role. While this shook her badly, she knew that her father would want her to move forward in her life. One of their most important shared qualities is a strong optimism. She embraced this optimistic viewpoint, finished her last assessment and got the job the next morning. She had 12 years at that company before she went out to begin consulting, and it was thanks to the lesson of optimism that she'd learned from her father.

From Corporate to Coaching

While Renee had a fantastic corporate career – even winning the national "Make a Difference" Award as a national business manager and sales associate – in the end corporate work stopped lighting her fire. She was leading a national team, writing and implementing programs and having a great deal of impact and success. But she knew that to truly help individuals and teams she needed to think bigger and broader. And she knew that what she really loved, and her favourite part of what she did, was the coaching aspect. So, she left the corporate world in favour of consulting and, ultimately, coaching.

Renee began building her own consulting practice under her personal brand. She started studying coaching, engaging her own coach to help her truly understand both sides of the work. This work embraced her really strong 'why' – which was to grow people, not because she was a manager, but because they were ready for it.

Getting the Basics Right

Like many consultants, when Renee first started her work, she was happily taking on anyone and everyone. She said that during her first year she would coach "cats, dogs, chairs, tables... anyone that would come into [her] vicinity". But over time, she began to niche down to the clients she could best help. And that meant getting the basics right.

> **"**
> *You don't build a business. You build people and people build the business.*

It was at this stage that we began working together. Renee was brilliant at what she does, but she needed a little help to get that message to more of the right people so it would cost her less time, energy and effort and she could gain more return for it.

Together we began to develop tiny habits that would help Renee's business to thrive from the bottom up.

The Power of Tiny Habits

When it comes to tiny habits, Renee's have been built to bolster her business in a way that honours who she is and the clients she is serving. While she sometimes does a myriad of different things in a day, she finds that clustering like-minded jobs, or "headspace zones" as she calls them, helps her to be more efficient, getting more done in a single day.

For example, if she's going to do a podcast, she might do five in one day in order to maximise her effectiveness. When it comes to sales calls, she sets herself a goal of five a day, and sticks to that religiously. She also commits to writing two blogs every fortnight at a minimum, which back up her "social media Sunday", the once-a-month time where she creates the content for her socials. And she's intentional about her bookings, ensuring she has one in the morning and one at the end of the day.

For Renee, she's found the most success by building tiny habits around different areas in her business and then bashing together all the like-minded roles and jobs. Of course, these elements are always flexibly shifting to take into account the directionality of her work and her clients' needs and even the world around her. For example, as many of us have also found in our own consulting roles, today Renee's work is about 50/50 virtual and face-to-face. This change meant changing the habits within her business as well. So, now when she does virtual work she ensures she has full days of virtual meetings or full days of face-to-face, which helps her to make the most out of both.

"Helping me to become who I am and who I'm continually becoming."

Renee believes that her corporate background gave her the push to do what she does now. In fact, she says it was those great roles that "helped me become who I am and who I'm continually becoming."

This corporate work was underpinned by the inherent values earned in her childhood, including her own optimistic approach in life. In fact, embracing an optimistic approach to her work is part of what defines Renee's success. And it's part of what helped her get to where she is today.

For example, she wrote her first book in 90 days. While it took the personal sacrifice of her time outside of regular business hours – time she'd normally spend relaxing with friends and family, doing yoga and cooking – she knew it would be worth it. She *optimistically* embraced the challenge and saw tremendous results because of it.

An Evolving Business

Like any business, Renee's has evolved over the years and it continues to evolve. Renee says that even in the recent years of her fully established business, she still finds that she attracts different types of clients over time. And she believes that this is the natural way – that over time you will begin to repel those clients that just aren't right for you or that you aren't able to help well while naturally drawing in those that you are.

While she isn't in the position of helping just anybody and everybody now (like in the beginning!) working with the right people means her business continues to grow and blossom. This organic metamorphosis shows that she's willing to surrender and be open to change to give her clients what they need and not just what she thinks they need.

Even when delivering leadership programs, the context will be different year on year, and the delivery needs will change. Being able to flexibly respond to that over time means that Renee's clients trust that she is giving them exactly the help and insight that they need. But to do that, she needed to embrace that openness of changing and saying, OK, well this is what we need to do now even when it's uncomfortable or difficult.

Renee Today

Renee's programs today have often been born out of the needs that she personally has had, as well as her own expertise, ideas and inspirations. But they've never lost sight of the clients that she serves. She puts her heart and soul into every single client, every single day. And she has designed and run over 3,000 workshops and programs on leadership and communication and conducted close to 2,500 coaching sessions. In each of these programs, and in her one-on-one coaching arm, Renee sees communication as the underlying essence of everything, while the workshops and coaching help to take groups and individuals into deep transformational pathways for growth and development.

Renee has also written three fantastic books. The first, *Limitless Leadership*, was designed to help leaders and organisations shift their leadership capabilities to lead from the inside out. She's also a contributor to the *Leaders of Influence* anthology. And in 2021 she published her third book, *Gift Mindset – Unwrap the 12 gifts to lead and live a life of purpose, connection and contribution.*

I know that many people in our community utilise her *Gift Mindset* book – which is so powerful and relevant today. Renee describes this book as her baby in this lifetime – and it shares 12 gifts that help the readers to lead and live a life of purpose, connection and contribution. Filled with insights, interviews, stories, case studies and tips, it's designed to help the readers adopt and embrace the gift mindset in life and in the workplace.

Gift Mindset has impacted on so many different people from teens to CEOs and from cafe owners to university professors. It's helped fuel their motivation and drive, to stay focused on being in service and being open to evolve. In today's world, it seems everyone is embracing this at some level.

I've spoken with Renee (putting her on the spot) about her own gifts in light of the gift mindset. I asked her what her biggest gifts have been and how she recognised them as gifts. Renee says discovering your gifts is about unwrapping them, learning their lessons and using them to grow and develop both personally and in your work. All the gifts fit in 12 buckets and are what she likes to call "life skills".

For herself, Renee believes that one of her gifts is the gift of resilience. She believes resilience is layered and uplifted by both gratitude and optimism, and she knows that this gift has bolstered and cheered her on through every challenge and opportunity that she's ever had. She believes that it's this gift that's allowed her business to grow.

It particularly helped her when she faced losing the bulk of her business due to COVID in 2020. At that time, most of her work was corporate face-to-face delivery and when COVID hit, that decreased by about 90%. And while that work is coming back, if it hadn't been for her gift of resilience she wouldn't have been able to shift and reposition herself and her business in order to persevere.

Renee also sees the gift of contribution within herself. She believes this echoes the human need, and she simply doesn't feel good unless she's in service and contributing. She believes that if she's aware of this and contributing from the heart, things will come.

Renee has surrounded herself with a support crew dotted with other optimists and those who have also been given the gift of resilience. This team (and her wonderful husband) has helped her during times when the challenges got tough, and helped to "light her up and put a pep in her step" as she calls it. They've also been able to step in with gifts of their own that complement her own gifts, skills and experience.

A Triple Threat

In the consulting industry many consultants tend to have one way they like to work. Either they like to create, like to deliver or like to sell. But having known Renee a long time, she's one of the few that finds all three satisfying. And she says it all starts with great content.

"I love thinking. I'm probably too much of an ideas person, really. But I believe the better the content, the fresher the content, the better programs I can write and deliver," says Renee. "And this is my point of difference."

Renee's advice is that we get back to basics – just as she did – and find what sets us apart. If we focus on this then we'll find creating easy. From there referrals will flow (as long as we're proactive) and selling will become easy. Delivering will become easy as well, because we'll have been creating around solving our customers and clients' problems and that means we'll have the answers and solutions that they're looking for.

Using habits to learn to do these things is important as well. "When I'm delivering face-to-face with clients, and hearing their problems, I write notes and that's what I go and write my blogs on. It's just those little chats when someone says, 'Hey, have you ever thought of this?' Or, 'Do you ever see this?'"

Listening. Hearing. And then taking action. Those are Renee's steps to success.

🔑 3 Key Learnings

1. **Stay focussed on the metrics that matter**: Renee has an incredible amount of energy. So it can mean it's easy to spin wheels as working can be a default. She spends time implementing her metrics to make sure she stays on track and focussed on the goals she is trying to achieve.

2. **Collaborate but at the right time**: Renee gains a lot of energy and momentum working with others. She is naturally giving, hardworking and a team player. She is also a great collaborator so it's important for her to collaborate with people who have a practice at the same stage as she has and are prepared to put the same amount of work in. Undertaking a small project before undertaking anything too big can be a good way to start.

3. **Get the right people around you**: Renee is great at relationships and building connections and she maintains those relationships over a long period. She is generous and gives her time to them and knows that if she needs help she can gain support, advice and insights as well.

Listen to the Jane Anderson Show Podcast, Episode 63 –
Business Coach for Bookkeepers, Renee Giarrusso

CHAPTER 7

Alena Bennett

CFO Coach

CREATING A COMMUNITY

Alena Bennett is a finance professional. But like many female consultants her true passion is people. After working as an accountant and auditor across Australia and the US, Alena realised there was more to finance than numbers. And what stood out to her, what really fulfilled her, was helping people.

Throughout her career, Alena noticed both the positive and negative impact that leadership had on performance and, in particular, on team performance. Through her work (which spanned auditing, finance, risk and communications) she quickly began to realise that to get the results you first had to get the culture right. Her passion was ignited as she started to show her peers the positive impact of treating your team right.

A Passion Ignited

Alena had a fantastic finance career, so she wasn't looking for a 'dream job'. But one day, it turned up out of the blue. It was while working in her finance executive role that she found herself a participant at a leadership strategy day. And it was here that she had the sudden epiphany that she was on the wrong side of the table. Rather than being a participant, she wanted to be the facilitator!

At the time, Alena was excelling in her finance career, beavering away and climbing the ranks, but always with her personal slant on focusing on the people aspect. But when she discovered that coaching, facilitating, training and speaking could be a career path for her, it was a future she couldn't unsee. She knew that this was a change that had to happen.

Her first step was to learn as much as she could about her new dream job. So, she eagerly asked the facilitator for a coffee, wanting to devour as much information as she could. In those conversations, and through connecting with others, she identified that, although she could do the technical things that it took to succeed in finance (and do them well), she truly flourished when it came to people, relationships and influence. She quickly came to realise that her energy and effort were best placed partnering alongside the astute finance professionals, who excelled with the technical side of their role, but wanted to amplify their impact and elevate their results with leadership skills. Her eyes had been opened to her own genius zone.

Overcoming Challenges

Alena spent the next year working in a project role, outside of the finance industry, where she could implement her new skills. However, after that year she realised she really wanted, and needed, to focus on working with finance professionals. She had walked in their shoes, knew their challenges and understood their deadlines and pressures. So, never being one to shy away from a challenge, she started her own practice as a leadership development and high performance coach, and began working with CFOs and finance leadership teams seeking next-level success.

Of course, like many consultants, she jumped in with both feet. As her practice grew, she became all the things—mentor, trainer, facilitator and coach—for her clients. And she found herself doing everything in her business as well. So, like many consultants, this became one of her greatest challenges. She needed to find a way to do less, while achieving more.

For Alena, delivering her services was always something that worked well for her. But she needed the support systems and processes around her. She says, 'I dare say that the delivery was good.... But as we know, delivery is just one piece of the pie. You also need the surrounding infrastructure to make it all happen.'

Make-or-Break Moments

Setting up the right support systems and processes for her business was the first step. But it wasn't the end of Alena's challenges. Balancing her family life, raising her daughters and being the main breadwinner continued to challenge her. She knew she'd hit on a winning recipe and found herself with a successful business. But to continue her success and give her family stability she needed to pull out the big guns. And this came in the guise of her writing a book for women in finance.

> *I dare say that the delivery was good.... But as we know, delivery is just one piece of the pie. You also need the surrounding infrastructure to make it all happen.*

Alena says, 'Women in finance often have a disconnect between their purpose and their number crunching, hyper-analytical jobs. They don't realise it until it's often too late... when their motivation has plateaued or, even worse, their performance is suffering.' Her book addressed this disconnect, immortalising everything she had discovered over the space of her career in plain black and white. It helped other women in finance to identify this purpose whether it aligned with their finance work or not.

Her book, *Meaning Matters: Results Beyond the Numbers*[1], was a game changer in a number of areas. The first was in her own confidence. Even though Alena knew it was full of good information, because she'd been teaching it for years, there was something about holding a book and knowing she'd written it. She knew that not everybody could (or would) be able to accomplish that. And she knew the book held fantastic substance and value for her readers.

---

1 Bennett, A., Phillips, M. (2019). Meaning Matters: Results Beyond the Numbers. Hambone Publishing.

Alena says, 'Like they say, you've got to sell yourself before you can sell to anyone else. But there was a realisation: I've written a book and gosh, there's actually lots of good stuff in here.'

Her book publication and the subsequent reviews speak for themselves. It was the validation she needed and gave her the impetus to go on. Soon she was asked to come and speak about her book, her strategies and her ethos. And now she is onto her second book and has added 'successful author' to her impressive resume.

Craving Community

Even with the determination, hard work and success behind running her own business, Alena felt that she was missing something—people. She simply didn't have the people, the team or the community around her that she craved. One day, after starting her own consulting practice, Alena stumbled upon a contract job. She knew she wanted back into a corporate setting, not because she didn't love her business, but because she was lonely. A feeling which I think most honest women in consulting may have felt at some stage.

She says, 'I was missing that energy, that mojo. I wanted to make sure that I was around good people, and I knew I needed a sense of community to thrive.'

With that thought in mind she accepted the contract role that she could run alongside growing her business. Being able to run her business alongside a contract job allowed her the best of both worlds and is not something Alena thinks is a failure but a huge help to continue to grow her practice. In fact many in our community juggle our own businesses with supplementary jobs for a variety of reasons—cash flow stability, a diversification of job risk or simply our own personality or internal drivers.

A Game Changing Moment—Cut Through Collaterals

Coinciding with the start of lockdown, Alena knew that it was time to take the next steps in her practice, and she wanted to use her time in lockdown wisely. So, she decided to invest in the Women with Influence online program, Cut Through Collaterals.

Alena says about the program, 'If I think about the trajectory of my business, that was the game changer'.

It helped her create 14 must-have documents (or collateral) that she needed to elevate her practice, including landing pages, white papers and brochures. These are all the elements that people never have (or take) the time to do. Yet, at the same time they are struggling to make their sales goals, struggling to get their price point up or struggling to articulate their value. And it's these documents that help you to meet those goals and share your value with others.

For Alena, having this collateral in place gave her ease and flow in her sales and in her practice, enabling her to continue to do it, and do it well. Meanwhile having the contract role helped support her because she had community (the people she worked with) and the added security of cash flow. For Alena, being able to work both in her business and in her community took away the potential negative energy that sometimes gets in your way when you know you're not where you want to be.

Doing It All with Intention

One of the biggest problems that many women in consulting struggle with is how to do it all, just as Alena did in the early days of her practice. While many women may feel compelled to start their practices and follow their purpose, they're often held back by the pressure to have a certain level of income. And they struggle to maintain that level of income while also balancing the momentum to progress their practices.

Alena's advice to push through and overcome that is to intentionally manage your energy. She says, 'Being in a community of high-achieving women, we all want to do the best in everything that we do. But be intentional with your energy. I knew I had to do a great job in my contract work, but I also knew that anything extra that I gave would actually be something that I took away from my own business.'

In fact, the work (and the balance) that Alena had put into her practice had paid off, and her success increased exponentially. This eventually made having it all—her own business and a contract—unmanageable. Although the decision to take the contract was the right one at the time, she ultimately allowed herself the space to reassess the situation. She gave herself permission to make a choice, and that was to move into her practice full time.

Creating Community for Success

Alena has found herself coming back to her roots by creating a signature program, called the CFO Boardroom, which centres around helping leaders – but particularly CFOs – build a community. Alena explains her intent to work with CFOs specifically because they are at the top of the tree, the ones that can have the most impact and influence, not only with their teams but at the leadership and organisation level.

The high-performance, 12-month coaching program brings CFOs together in a safe and genuine environment. It includes quarterly masterminds and one-on-one coaching and, of course, provides that vital community that Alena herself had craved. Certainly, it's not for the faint-hearted. It's for those who are high achievers looking to continue to elevate, push themselves and move out of the back office to be seen as a real value-creator for the business.

Over 12 months Alena built up her list of CFOs from 64 to over 800 and cites consistency, rigour and discipline as the key to getting out there. She currently has a group of 10 CFOs on the $20,000, 12-month program. And her commitment to productivity, and having great systems in place, allow her to deliver to her community. Next on her to-do list is in-person events, in particular an annual 'CFO of the Future' community event which will bring all of her CFOs and aspiring CFOs together yearly.

Alena describes her work as 'bringing the smartest financial minds together'. But she also adds that she is 'fundamentally dealing with a bunch of human beings with complex lives that just want to be good. They want to be there for their friends, their families and their loved ones, which is something that binds us all really.'

What Would She Have Done Differently?

Like most things in life and business, it has been a journey for Alena to get where she is today. She believes if she was to have her time over, she would spend time thinking about what she really wanted and be less swayed by what other people may have offered. Advice is often given out, but self-awareness is key to success.

Her advice is to stay in your lane and, as hard as it is, not compare yourself to others. Alena says, 'Be comfortable with the fact there are going to be people that are ahead of you or that are doing different things that look more fun and sexier than you. But play your own game, and you'll succeed.'

Alena encourages women with their own practices to invest in themselves early and find a mentor they resonate with. Reinforcement, trust, access to networks and guidance from sources such as Cut Through Collateral have resulted in fast-tracked success and have, quite frankly, transformed her practice.

🔑 3 Key Learnings

1. Don't be afraid to niche. Naturally we want to help everyone, but it actually doesn't help anyone if you just try to be all things to all the people.
2. Live with intention. Make your decisions for a reason and reassess them if they no longer work for you.
3. Think about who. It's about more than the revenue or the take home. It's about the people you work with. Care enough to be obsessed with solving their particular issues and problems.

Listen to the Jane Anderson Show Podcast, Episode 61,
Director & Executive Leadership Consultant, CFO Mentor,
Chartered Accountant, Author, Alena Bennett

CHAPTER 8

Jessica Giles

Money Expert

MASTERY AND MINDSET

Jessica Giles is an accountant by trade. But her real area of expertise is money mastery. Jessica is a money mastery manifestation law of attraction coach, and her philosophy is based around embracing the masculine force of money management systems, combined with the feminine aspects of mindset. She believes this is a force to be reckoned with. And I think she's right.

But before you start believing that money management comes easy to Jessica, she firmly believes that she didn't 'come out of the box' this way. In fact, she's so passionate about coaching women in this space because this was not the original trajectory of her life. She had to learn every aspect of it the hard way.

From High School Dropout to Money Master

Jessica dropped out of high school at the age of 16, and started her career working in a local petrol station. But over time, she realised that she wanted more for her life. So she started taking accounting at her local adult education centre. For someone who never loved school, no one was more surprised than she was when she fell in love with the role and the industry. But this was the push she needed, and after working through the subjects at her local centre, she headed off to get her university degree as well.

Of course, like many women, this time of her life coincided with having her children. And when she sat her university exams, it was with a screaming newborn outside. But Jessica continued to embrace her philosophy, 'It doesn't matter where you've come from. It only matters where you're going.'

Not Your Average Bookkeeper

Once Jessica finished school, she was ready to start her bookkeeping and accounting practice. And it was during these early years that she realised that clients weren't just handing over their receipts to her. They were also handing over their financial power.

> *Often business owners and consultants find themselves lost when it comes to their finances. This makes them feel vulnerable and insecure and even, sometimes, ashamed. This insecurity and shame in one part of the business can flow on into the other parts, eroding confidence and resilience.*

She saw that most people she worked with had started their business or practice because they were passionately invested in what they did—in their own sphere of expertise—but that this passion didn't always equate to sound financial management skills. Many of them simply didn't have the knowledge to grow a profitable business, and were running an expensive hobby, instead.

Often business owners and consultants find themselves lost when it comes to their finances. This makes them feel vulnerable and insecure and even, sometimes, ashamed. This insecurity and shame in one part of the business can flow on into the other parts, eroding confidence and resilience, despite being brilliant in the other parts of their business.

Around the same time, Jessica had what she calls a 'spiritual awakening'. This occurred when she found herself a single mum very suddenly. She knew she had to change her own perceptions and her own beliefs, so she started to bring everything that she was learning about mindset and manifestation into her work. This was the catalyst to a huge transformation in not just her business, but also the business and success of her clients.

Because it's not about your relationship with money or your finances, it doesn't matter what these have looked like to this point. But it is very much about understanding what you're choosing and what you're making available for moving forward.

Jessica was ready to help her clients take control of their finances. But she still had to overcome some challenges first.

Overcoming Imposter Syndrome

Like many other women, Jessica sometimes grappled with imposter syndrome feelings. Even after finding a great deal of success within her business, despite having been engaged to speak Australia-wide, coaching clients all over the world and writing a book, there was still a little part of Jessica that felt trapped in her 16-year-old body working at the petrol station.

Imposter syndrome is an insidious thing. In 2020 I took a survey of the experts in my community, and a full 30% reported feeling the sting of imposter syndrome. *Harvard Business Review* defines imposter syndrome as doubting your abilities and feeling like a fraud.[1] But most importantly, it goes on to say that it disproportionately affects high-achieving people. And that was exactly the situation for Jessica.

When Jessica and I began working together, it became clear pretty quickly that we needed to tackle her imposter syndrome and help her to have more confidence while articulating her value. Because she *was* bringing incredible value to her customers. In fact, one of Jessica's best traits is that she knew her customers so well, and she was able to demonstrate this to them.

---

1   Tulshyan, R. and Burey, J. (11 February 2021). 'Stop Telling Women They Have Imposter Syndrome'. *Harvard Business Review*. Accessed at https://hbr.org/2021/02/stop-telling-women-they-have-imposter-syndrome.

When people worked with Jessica they were impressed by how strong she is as a person, how smart and switched on, but also how incredibly *nice* she is. They never felt that she would judge them, or look down on them in any way, and a lot of this was down to her background and the challenges she'd faced herself.

Jessica's customers trust her. They felt safe with her. And they found her extremely likeable and almost disarming. It was the perfect recipe for money mastery success. But Jessica just needed to believe this herself.

Working with me, Jessica was able to articulate her value to herself. And while imposter syndrome is always there, potentially rearing its head (something that is also true for many of us!), Jessica now understands and fully believes that fear is a one-trick pony. And when you face it you drive it away.

This is part of breaking down the stories that you've been telling yourself, and now this is part of Jessica's superpower. Because she knows about imposter syndrome, because she talks so openly about being a high school dropout and a single mum, she's able to help her clients see beyond their own perceived limitations. She's able to help lift them up, elevate them, even within their financial spheres and within their lives generally. When they work with her, they don't feel disempowered, embarrassed or ashamed, but precisely the opposite.

Sadly, Jessica faced a relationship breakdown and on the day that Jessica became a single mum she didn't immediately turn around to try to take on the world. But she did embrace the philosophy that when she had healed from this, she was going to use it to help others. And she did.

Interestingly, many of the women she helped were not just single mums, but were wanting to become single mums. They were looking for ways to escape a bad relationship or situation but they needed to know that they were going to be OK. They needed to be financially independent so they could manage their own lives. Jessica supports women to be financially empowered so they can make the right decisions and support themselves whether they're in or out of a relationship. In fact the relationship and the money could become two separate things.

Uncovering the Money Story

Today Jessica's clients see her as a breath of fresh air. Not just because of her personality and her youthful exuberance, but also because she brings new insight to old problems.

Her clients have often been 'educated' by their former accountants. In other words, they've been told in no uncertain terms all the things they're doing wrong and how they could be doing things better and making so much more money. But at the end of the day, this just leaves them feeling disempowered and lost. And it justifies the money story they've been telling themselves.

Jessica believes that every person has a story when it comes to money. This could have been carried from generation to generation or be something that comes to you alone. It could be the story that 'I'm not good with money.' Or, 'People like me don't have money.' Or, 'Money's hard to come by.' Or, even, 'Why would someone pay me to do this job?'

All this is carried through, not only in how we manage our business finances, but also in the strategies we use to grow a profitable business, and in how we price and sell ourselves. And while we like to think that we just have a money strategy problem, in fact it's all about our mindset, the stories we tell around our money mindset and belief system that we're carrying.

So, for many people, they may not feel they deserve to earn $50,000 a month. Or if they do, they may feel it was a fluke or anomaly. Or they may feel that they should be limited to what they earned in their corporate life or constrained to the lifestyle their parents lived. This isn't an outright belief, but part of the mindset of what they believe inside about themselves. The story they're telling, and their belief in it.

The Yin and the Yang

For many of Jessica's clients, they were caught in the web of wanting to create, or wanting to work in their business. The details of the numbers and the finances were getting lost for them. But Jessica's approach was to bring the left brain, or masculine energy, around systems and processes (the bottom line) together with the feminine energy of the mindset and manifestation of what her clients really wanted and needed (the top line). You can think of it as the yin and yang of money. And neither works well without the other.

The Money Mindset

For Jessica, money mindset starts with two things.

The first, is realising that you aren't going to step out of the blocks straight away and command a premium price for your offering. Those who have the best money mindset understand that this is a process and that they'll have to regularly expand themselves through that process. This is the first half of a fantastic money mindset. And if you can grasp this practice, then you can have love, gratitude and celebration within yourself for doing so.

> *The more you focus on the value that you're delivering, the more you're able to transform your clients and your community.*

The second is to take the focus off selling yourself. When we think about selling ourselves, that's when all the stories end. Instead, you have to take yourself out of the picture, and separate yourself just a little bit. The more you focus on the value that you're delivering, the more you're able to transform your clients and your community.

Jessica believes that once you've taken these first all-important steps you'll be in a good position to start to shift the energy, and then get that energy into motion, moving you towards something else, something better, within the universe. And though it may feel awkward in those first wobbly moments, that's good. Because that's where the real growth happens, as long as you're willing to take those steps. And it's important to remember that everyone has money blocks. There are people being paid millions of dollars who still wonder, just a little bit, if they're worth it.

Once her clients get into that motion and start offering their services and connecting with people, then they're in that positive feedback loop. They start seeing their impact, and their results. And the more they see it, the easier it is to see it the next time. They begin to feel that affirmation and feel a connection to their worth.

Your Relationship With Money

Today Jessica takes all her learnings, experience, life challenges and results from working both with me and on her own to encourage her clients to think about their relationship with money like any other relationship. Jessica believes however that, unlike a boyfriend or a partner, money is there for life. And like any other relationship we're often thinking about how we feel about money, especially when there's not enough of it, or when it doesn't stick around or grow.

> 66
>
> *When it comes to money mastery, remember that everyone has money blocks.*

Her challenges with confidence and imposter syndrome have let Jessica see first-hand that when money mindset operates from a place of fear then, even when there's money coming into your business, the energy will still be one of worry and desperation. You will always just be thinking, 'I need another client. I need money.' This energy is going to keep you tied down to the same space you've always been in.

She challenges her clients to query their own relationships with money to help switch that perspective. Now the relationship is no longer about need, or desperation, or resentment, but about gratitude and abundance. And once you start that shift, then you can start to mirror this in your physical existence as well.

What Would Jessica Do Differently?

Of course, despite the successes and the learnings that have come from her unique challenges, there are still some things that Jessica advises others to do differently if they can. Jessica tells her children and her nephews that they should stay in school, and avoid the same sometimes-difficult route that she took. But when it really comes down to it, she wouldn't change anything about her career trajectory. Jessica believes that her life has been shaped by the experiences that she's had. And they allow her to support her clients and her community in a way she wouldn't have been able to otherwise.

But she does wish that she'd addressed her identity and self-worth issues earlier, and not focused so much on pure business building. Because, as Jess says, 'The strategy is only as good as the person behind it'.

Giving Clients the Gift of Themselves

At the end of the day Jessica doesn't consider herself a guru or leader when it comes to the work she does. In fact, she believes that the biggest gift she gives to her clients is the gift of themselves. She helps them to connect with themselves and find the answers for themselves, because we know from our own stories and experiences that being told something doesn't connect you. Reaching awareness for themselves is where the real transformation happens.

🔑 3 Key Learnings

1. Challenges create opportunities to learn. Embrace them. Grow from them.

2. Imposter syndrome affects many high-achievers. Do the work to articulate your value and see what you bring to the table for your customers. This will let you overcome the lack of confidence and fear that drives imposter syndrome.

3. When it comes to money mastery, remember that everyone has money blocks. There are people being paid millions of dollars who still wonder if they're worth it. Work to uncover your own money stories, so you can move past them and into financial freedom.

Listen to the Jane Anderson Show Podcast, Episode 59–
Accountant & Certified Money Coach Jessical Giles

CHAPTER 9

Ally Nitschke

Courageous Leadership Expert

HAVING A PLAN

Leadership expert Ally Nitschke is a specialist in courageous conversations. But she wasn't always so courageous. In fact, when she first entered the world of thought leadership, she wondered, 'Who's going to pay attention to little old me from little old Adelaide?'

But what came next was a major mindset shift: finding out she made it into the top five podcasts in the country as host of *Made For More*, where she unpacks her expertise in leadership, mindset, courage and goal setting. Now she is a speaker, educator, trainer, coach, mentor and – with her first book on the way – a soon-to-be author.

With an incredible practice, on an extraordinary trajectory, Ally lets us in on how having a plan can elevate your results.

Multi-Tasking Mama

Many new mums might find themselves in a milky, sleep-deprived blur during those first few months of having a newborn. But not Ally. When her youngest of four boys was just six weeks old, Ally was already thinking about the future of her career and making the decision to launch her own practice.

With a background working across many different industries and sectors including banking, finance and the federal government, she realised that the nine-to-five juggle was not what she wanted. Nor was it designed for women in the workplace.

> **"**
> *People are most effective when they have the confidence and competence to develop healthy relationships, the bases of which are built on openness, achievement and good communication.*

She felt under-utilised and decided that her skills would be better spent inspiring people and helping them believe they are 'made for more'. This was the seeds of her new consultancy business.

As managing director of Made for More, Ally offers workshops, programs and coaching to equip her clients with the confidence and clarity they need to raise the bar and be the best they can be. The business aims to develop high-performing leaders who are both empathetic and courageous, while also avoiding stress and burnout.

Her flagship program, Courageous Leaders, shares leadership strategies like leaning into tough conversations, setting a clear vision and developing a road map to get there. Ally and her team believe that people are most effective when they have the confidence and competence to develop healthy relationships, the bases of which are built on openness, achievement and good communication.

Entering the Thought Leadership Sphere

A year into her business, Ally attended a local Professional Speakers Association event in Adelaide. 'It was really my introduction into the whole idea of thought leadership,' Ally says. After being told her entire life that she 'had too many ideas' or to 'calm down and focus on one thing', when she finally heard the magical phrase, 'yes, develop your ideas!', she felt like she was home.

Working on developing her ideas, getting them out into the world and having the courage to speak about them was when things really started to elevate. As Ally developed her own content and started getting into a rhythm publishing her weekly newsletters on LinkedIn, she soon started to experience a promising shift. People began to approach her, saying they had read an article she wrote or heard a podcast she was a guest on, and wanted to work with her.

Narrowing in on courageous conversations is a vital job, given that the research says seven out of 10 people will simply avoid a tough conversation.[1] And his conversation gap is leading to decreased engagement, lost productivity and higher staff turnover as people ultimately decide to just quit, rather than speaking up.[2]

Ally's podcast explores the concept of courageous conversations further, as she interviews a range of people who share fascinating stories of challenge, finding courage and leadership. In doing so, Ally has built a whole bank of knowledge and advanced thinking around courage.

The Snowball Effect

Ally has experienced tremendous success with a top-five podcast, selling out five-figure programs that greatly improve the culture within organisations. She attributes her success to a snowball effect that came from mastering confidence in her content by unpacking her ideas, unlocking her worth and valuing her own expertise, via our community.

'For a long time, my internal monologue wasn't helpful. I'd tell myself I was brand new, what did I think I was doing? Then I realised I had actually been doing this for more than 20 years!'

Our community of consultants helped her to see her own value and embrace that, to set her along her path and develop her plan.

---

1   Gilchrist, K. (14 March 2019). '7 in 10 Americans are avoiding difficult conversations at work – here's how to tackle them'. yahoo!finance. Accessed at https://finance.yahoo.com/news/7-10-americans-avoiding-difficult-014850865.html.
2   Gilchrist (2019).

Implementing Strategy

The regular process of showing up, getting into a rhythm and putting a strategy in place has helped Ally sit in the driver's seat of her practice, instead of being part of a reactive process of 'just taking orders'. She has taken the IP, the collateral and all the brochures around the products and programs that she sells and has started thinking beyond day rates.

Taking feedback on her strategies from our community has helped her push through, but she admits that in the early days she didn't really have a plan. And that made it hard to realise her value.

Realising Her Value

When it comes to realising her value, it didn't happen all at once.

'I would love to say that it's been an overnight shift,' she says. 'But it has been teeny-tiny, incremental steps the entire way.'

Ally has had the right people – including mentoring and community – around her to remind her of her own worth and encourage her to nudge up her rates. But over time, having her plan has allowed her to build her confidence and do just that.

Of course, it's been a learning process for Ally to feel worthy of positive feedback, rather than simply brushing it off as many of us do. She recently ran a program for a group of leaders from divisions across an organisation and, when it concluded, one of the most experienced leaders present took Ally aside and told her it was the best leadership program she had ever done.

'I've decided to start taking some of those compliments at face value and recognising that actually I'm having a huge impact. And that's the whole aim of the game – to impact leaders,' she says.

This shift in learning to listen to and accept such positive feedback has encouraged Ally to understand her worth and increase her rates. She now rejects the clients who won't meet her price levels and has been stretching her thinking into how she can package her program offerings differently to add more value.

Today, Ally obsesses about her customers. She talks so deeply about the world that her clients are in and the problems or experiences they're having, but also the opportunities that are here for them. So instead of thinking in terms of selling a simple, short program, it can be wise to consider what the root of the problem is that you're trying to solve. What is the bigger issue you can help your client base to work through? And what journey do you need to articulate to take them on that?

By focusing on the end result you might realise that instead of one day, it may need to be a longer program, for example, one month or even longer. Or you may learn to recognise the value of marketing your program across the wider business so that you can offer your value to a greater number of leaders. That process (or understanding your end result) will help you to add intrinsic value to your offerings.

> *The regular process of showing up, getting into a rhythm and putting a strategy in place has helped Ally sit in the driver's seat of her practice, instead of being part of a reactive process of 'just taking orders'.*

The Thrill of the Stage

The seeds of Ally's love of public speaking were sown back in the days before she embarked on her 'real work'. Back then she was a professional ballet dancer who thrived on the anticipation and excitement of performing on stage. A little later, when she was in her early leadership years, Ally confided in her development coach at the time that she wanted to be a motivational speaker, and she was met with resistance.

She says, 'They were like, "Well, you will never be able to do that right now. You need more experience, and you don't have any life stories." But I thought, "Oh, I've done quite a bit in my short amount of time."'

Her journey has now come full circle, as she's conquered that stage to share her truths. She says that she's in her element when public speaking and loves the high of coming off the stage. She believes it's important to bang as many great things into your keynote as possible without overwhelming people. And being able to share her message with a huge audience, having the chance to trigger some different thinking or some sort of action, still feels remarkable to this girl from Adelaide.

Ally has also embraced the brand-positioning benefits that come from delivering a speech. She says the flow-on effects that happen after a speaking appearance are great for her practice.

'I'm there to do a 45-minute keynote. But the next minute, [I'm] hearing from the person I was sitting next to at the event's sister's cousin, who is in Sydney, who has heard about it and wants to talk,' she says. It's a wonderful way to position yourself.

Making the Most of Opportunities

Ally has delivered plenty of talks over the years and says she now kicks herself for all of the lost opportunities. Before she realised the importance of building her list, she would give a great speech and receive great feedback, but then never connect with the attendees again. 'So having a bit of a strategy going in there has been a real game changer,' she explains. 'And it's made me, I guess, think about where I want people to go and what I want them to do and take away after the event.'

Ally says she now understands how important it is to get the people in the audience who are connecting with her added to her list, so she can keep engaging with them through weekly newsletters. She now has either an opt-in or an SMS burst or mentions 'Hey, I do a Daily Dose of Courage.'

She says, 'It's crucial to keep the connection going with the ones who are curious and want to know more. If a speaker has elevated their thinking, they will be keen to access more of your information.'

Ally says that speaking is not for everybody. But she feels that if you can work out your version of that, then it makes sense to go out and speak to audiences you may not have crossed paths with otherwise, to share your message and build your list in that way.

Effort Leads to Rewards

Ally recommends listening to 'The Echo of Life' episode of *The Ed Mylett Show* podcast, where the business leader and keynote speaker explains that the things you do today will have an echo that will come back to you. So essentially, whatever effort you're putting in now, you'll see the benefits and reap the rewards of that at some stage in the future.

Ally says she keeps this concept in mind whenever she's working in the thought leadership space and running her own business. She chooses to put in the effort now for tomorrow's benefit.

She says, 'When's the best time to plant a tree? 20 years ago. When's the best time to do the work? Right now.'

Just as Ally has done, if nothing's happening in your business, make something happen. Don't sit around and wait and complain that it's not happening – do something. Ally has put this into practice by creating events for her ideal clients to attend, sharing IP, hosting a podcast, releasing a regular newsletter and even writing a book.

Get Support Where You Need It

Ally has been able to achieve so much in her work life while also being an amazing mum to four little boys. But of course, it hasn't always been easy. In the past 12 months she has also been clever enough to bring on some support. She has begun to delegate tasks, engaged people like virtual assistants and has now started to get some efficient systems in place. By having people who can backfill her 'weak spots', she is free to carry out the creative work she loves.

'I do have an incredible team who are good at all the things that I'm not good at. I think this is a really important thing – to find people who fill your gaps.'

Ally says she is not interested in learning how to systemise or automate or enter data, nor is she interested in attention to detail. She prefers to engage people who love those tasks, which means she has time to focus on the work that lights her up.

She also says that having a husband who supports her and shares the workload at home makes a world of difference to her work/life balance as a working mum.

'I know that's not the case for everyone. So just to caveat, I don't do all of the things all of the time. I have people around me who are incredible.'

Ally's Best Tips

Ally's advice to anyone who is at the same stage she was at 12 months ago is, firstly, to find the right mentor or coach. She jumped in early on, but she suggests finding someone who is doing what you're doing, and doing it at an exceptional level.

Secondly, she recommends getting out of your own echo chamber and building a community around you. She suggests having people on your advisory panel who can stretch you, rather than those who haven't elevated their thinking. 'When you're going, "Holy moly woah," then you probably found the right people to go "Yeah, I want to hang out with them a little bit more."'

According to Matt Church, founder of Thought Leaders Business School, when it comes to the number of people in your tribe, the magic numbers are 15, 150, 1,500 and 15,000. The first 15 people in your tribe are those closest to you. These are your advisors and mentors who challenge you to stretch, elevate and grow. These are the people that you need to bring into your community. And these are the people that Ally has built around her.

Thirdly, she suggests having cadence and rhythm in place – whether it's your cadence on newsletters or on publishing resources. She proposes choosing just five things a day to get done in order to be the most efficient and focused.

Ally says, 'We tend to, as women particularly, write huge to-do lists that take longer to write than they do to execute. So just focus on what's important.' Prioritising your most important tasks is essential. 'Hot tip: email's not one of [the five],' she adds.

🔑 3 Key Learnings

1. Building your list is more important than you think – have a web strategy in place.
2. Listen to and embrace positive feedback.
3. Find staff who fill your weaknesses.

Listen to the Jane Anderson Show Podcast, Episode 62 – Leadership Expert, Courageous Conversations Specialist, Speaker, Author, Ally Nitschke

CHAPTER 10

Cheryle Walker

Connected Leadership Expert

OVERCOMING THE IMPOSTER

While Cheryle Walker's official job title is consultant, facilitator and instructional designer of LIVE Online workshops, webinars and events, it really should be something along the lines of corporate clairvoyant or intuitive entrepreneur.

When the pandemic pulled the Australian workforce out of offices and pushed them into home-based and remote work, Cheryle had already spent years building a business that helped companies keep their employees connected, even when they were physically apart.

This virtual-world wizard suddenly found her expertise in high demand as the world's workers navigated a lonely new reality working from home. Her 20 years of experience designing and facilitating virtual classrooms, and her proficiency using web-conferencing software and online collaboration platforms to help others communicate, teach, learn and engage, was of massive value to companies managing remote teams for the first time.

But recognising this value herself didn't come naturally to Cheryle.

Corporate Beginnings

Cheryle first recognised the potential for virtual learning during her time with National Australia Bank. She spent almost a decade setting up digital learning strategy and channels for the bank, creating new roles for herself along the way. She saw a great opportunity to equalise the learning experience for the huge number of employees who were spread across the country. So whether you were in far western Queensland or Sydney, you would have the same opportunity to connect, network, learn and rub shoulders with people in the organisation.

Changing Attitudes and Opening Minds

Cheryle left the bank in 2013 to launch LIVE Online and share her secrets for smooth operating virtual classrooms and webinars. In the seven years leading up to COVID-19, she consistently met with the same resistance, regardless of who the client was.

They'd say, 'We don't want to do this.' Or, 'This won't work.' Or, 'My bandwidth is no good.' Cheryle knew that the clients were coming from a deficit mindset but they simply couldn't believe that digital learning could be just as good as face-to-face.

Cheryle's mission was to convince these companies that her concept could be just as good as in-person learning and even more engaging than static e-learning, as it was live and collaborative. But it was an uphill battle. It required her to hold hands, have tough conversations and consistently strive to change attitudes.

The learning curve for her clients went beyond just accepting the value and efficacy of virtual learning. It also involved the learning curve that happens while participating in virtual learning. And Cheryle spent a good deal of time guiding clients to bring their best, authentic selves forward rather than shutting down as soon as they were in front of the webcam. It was a slow process.

COVID-19 Changes Everything

Although Cheryle has been working in this space for 18 years, the last two years has seen her business experience phenomenal growth as a result of COVID-19 and the way we now work.

'All of a sudden, the pandemic comes along and people are ringing me up saying, "Well, now this is all we've got. And we know that you've been banging on about this for a long time!"' she says.

Clients were experiencing travel restrictions and lockdowns but still facing deadlines, and therefore had to pivot and deliver their programs in brand-new ways. Those who had always delivered face-to-face learning suddenly had to learn how to be confident and natural in front of a camera, as well as get across the new technology. Fortunately, Cheryle was on hand to guide them through the entire process.

Cheryle's business went boom. Instead of her reaching out to find clients as she had always done, suddenly they were piling onto her. In many ways this was great. But it also presented a lot of challenges. Not only did she need to manage this rapid rate of growth, but she also had to deal with a new level of competition. And she had to face one of her biggest struggles yet – overcoming imposter syndrome.

The Threat of Competition

As the whole world shifted to working from home, it was only natural that more and more people started following Cheryle's lead. These new competitors began offering services focused on running remote teams and webinars. In a (virtual) space that had been relatively quiet, suddenly there were experts everywhere.

Cheryle says, 'I felt fear about that. I thought all of a sudden, everybody can do what I can do.'

Of course, very few had the years of experience and the deep level of expertise that Cheryle possessed. As she looked deeper into her own work history, she realised that all of her stories and experiences working with clients across a range of industries and helping them to learn and grow, was a huge selling point.

Looking back at her achievements gave her another step up in confidence and reduced her fear of being 'vanilla' or being an imposter. Her clients, seeing her expertise, helped her to begin to see it as well. And she started to understand that just because others do what she does, it doesn't mean they do it any better than her or that she was any less worthy. But she still had a ways to go.

Fear of Success

Cheryle also realised that she feared success because she thought she wasn't worthy of it. Every time she delivered great results for her clients and they spoke highly about her work, her thoughts would jump to fears around not being good enough. And she would feel the burden of good recommendations leading to high expectations. She worried about what her expertise was and if she could deliver what was expected from her. Sound familiar?

Appreciating Her Own Worth

Cheryle and I worked on strategies to help her understand her own value and expertise. She needed to mine the depth of what she had achieved in her work, focus on that and put it out there to share with the world.

She began with a white paper that clearly laid out the value that she and her services could bring to a client. Then she wrote a book, *Leverage LIVE Online: How to create transformational engagement in webinars, virtual workshops and online meetings*,[1] which helped her to appreciate all of the experience and expertise she held in her niche area of work.

'When you work unpacking your own brain… it provides an enormous confidence level foundation of "I have done this and I've done that, too. And I achieved that and that client saw that value and achieved that as a result of what I did,"' Cheryle explains. 'And, ultimately, clarity leads to confidence.'

Until that point, she had carried all her knowledge in her head as she hopped around from client to client. But this year she focused on putting it on paper and unpacking it, repacking it, telling stories about it, framing it and creating metaphors from it. This process has helped her to understand different value perspectives on her work, whether it be the client perspective, end user perspective or her own perspective.

Writing these resources also helped her to realise the direction she wanted her business to be heading. Instead of simply responding to the needs of the market,

---

1   Walker, C. (2021). Leverage LIVE Online: How to create transformational engagement in webinars, virtual workshops and online meetings. BookPOD.

it was time for her to steer the ship. The white paper and her book, *Leverage LIVE Online*, were the collateral she needed to spur on more growth for her business.

Being Deliberate and Disciplined

When we don't know where our value lies in business, we can often resort to playing defence, or 'order taking'. When Cheryle needed to source more work, she would simply contact clients and see what they needed, then give a quote for the specific project and hope they accepted.

Now, she has learned to be more deliberate about her practice, by developing resources and programs that she can offer at a fixed cost. She describes this as 'being on the front foot' in terms of what she does and what she offers. Because she knows her own worth, she feels confident in her fees and rates, and is comfortable with the value she has built into her programs and services.

> **"**
>
> *Knowing your value can help you create a great value proposition and reassure you there's no need to drop your price.*

In the past, if a prospective client said her cost was too high, she admits she would have plummeted her rates to keep the work. But now that she understands her true value, she can accept the loss. She's even developed a network of LIVE Online experts who she can recommend when she is too busy or too expensive to take the work.

Cheryle has found that knowing your value can help you create a great value proposition and reassure you there's no need to drop your price.

Trusting in Your Expertise

Sticking to her core offering rather than 'order taking' has also helped Cheryle's business maintain its sense of identity, rather than catering to every prospective client that crosses the threshold. She has found the confidence in her own expertise to share her genuine advice with clients instead of simply following their lead.

Sometimes clients who are new to the virtual space don't always know what to ask for. Or they may request a service that wouldn't be as effective as something else. Cheryle now has the conviction in her own abilities to speak up and offer valuable advice as a consultant, rather than just taking the order.

Controlling the Rollercoaster Revenue

A side effect of 'order taking' in business is the financial uncertainty that can come with it. Cheryle felt like she was always at the mercy of clients and projects coming in, and constantly worried that business would fade away when the next slump hit. Whether it was a project ending, clients being away on holidays or the annual slow period over Christmas, the rollercoaster revenue was a constant stress.

Instead of being blindly responsive to the market, Cheryle now adopts intelligent forecasting to see what the market might need. She forward plans and makes sure she has a program, book or white paper ready to hook in the client no matter (or because of) what's going on in the market and world around her.

This change of strategy has seen her experience at least 60% growth in revenue. And she shows no signs of stopping.

Manageable Growth

Cheryle has her parents to thank for her entrepreneurial spirit, but also her wariness of running a small business. In the case of both parents, she saw the business overwhelm them and threaten to drown them. So naturally she is apprehensive about allowing the same thing to happen to her. As part of that she was fearful of employing people and growing her business to a size that would feel like a burden.

Cheryle's anxieties around business growth and sustaining employees' wages were tested recently as she took a giant step forward by employing her husband in her business. She has had to learn the delicate dance of differentiating between work that she needs to do and work that can be entrusted to someone else. As many business owners who have hired employees will know, it's no easy feat documenting your ingrained knowledge into systems and processes for others to follow. But once the hard task is done, delegating the routine work to leave you free to play in your genius is well worth it.

At the end of the day, Cheryle needed others to support her and her business so that scaling became manageable.

Words of Wisdom

What advice would Cheryle share with someone who is now where she was 12 months ago in her business? In other words, they have a good client base, but need to grow their confidence in order to grow their business.

'Do the positioning and the work, and the mindset will come,' she says. Cheryle spent a long time telling herself that when she felt confident she would write a book. Or when she lost the fear of success she would be ready to grow her practice. But after working together and being part of my community, she realised that she couldn't sit around waiting to be in the right headspace, she just needed to dive in head-first.

Once she had unpacked and mined the depth of her expertise, and shared everything she knew, she realised it had brought her into the mindset of being confident and knowing her own worth. She says that writing about what you do and being generous with clients was what worked for her.

> *Do the positioning and the work, and the mindset will come.*

'I just had to get in and get mucky with it. And it didn't take very long before, all of a sudden, I realised, wow, I think I can actually do this.'

Future Goals

Cheryle has come so far. She's learned how to trust her own thinking and fully appreciate the value and transformational experience she offers her clients. She has bought a beach house (which she often works from) and her dream car.

Her big dream now is to achieve total clarity on her expertise and the programs she offers. While she feels that things are a lot clearer than in the past, she is working to get crystal clear on her niche in the industry so she can have fewer distractions.

She says, 'I think you can be at your maximum effective level if you are clear about who you are, what you do and how you help. If you can say, "Let me help you; let me guide you," I think that's real leadership in your field.'

🔑 3 Key Learnings

1. Don't wait to feel confident. Do activities that create confidence.
2. Be intentional about how you develop your business, rather than just 'order taking'.
3. Unpacking your own expertise will help you overcome imposter syndrome.

Listen to the Jane Anderson Show Podcast, Episode 66, Remote Leadership Expert, Author, Coach, Cheryle Walker

CHAPTER 11

Michelle Bihary

Corporate Wellness Expert

EMPOWERING YOUR SUPPORT

We've all been there – stuck in a job where the workplace culture is uninspiring, pessimistic, or even downright destructive. It's disheartening and demeaning, and certainly isn't a formula for bringing out your best work.

Michelle Bihary is on a noble mission to reshape our working environments. She believes that people are an organisation's greatest asset, and when they feel supported and safe, they will bring the very best versions of themselves to the workplace.

Of course, Michelle didn't always feel so passionate about the workplace. It took a firsthand experience seeing these poor leadership practices at play in a former workplace to really motivate her to dip her toes into the world of leadership training. But once she got a glimpse of the benefits of a fantastic workplace environment, she knew this was the space where she needed to be.

The Disheartening Reality of Many Workplaces

For many years prior to shifting her focus to leadership training, Michelle worked as a mental health professional specialising in adolescent and youth mental health. In her role as team leader and manager, she was astonished by how often evidence about leadership, mentoring and workforce wellbeing was ignored. This was particularly surprising since her workplace was an evidence-based clinical practice whose foundations were research and science. Yet, the 'science' of leadership was never really explored.

In fact, some of the organisation's systems were the opposite to what was known to bring out the best in employees. Rather than helping their employees to perform well, relate effectively and learn, they were sub-optimal – employees felt shut down and stressed out. 'I saw some very poor, below-the-line leadership practices that were completely at odds with what we knew about bringing out the best in people and creating psychological safety within our therapy work,' she says.

It's a sad irony that Michelle's workplace was committed to creating psychological safety for its clients, yet disregarded the fact that its employees—its people—needed to feel safe to thrive at work. Employees need a healthy workplace ecosystem to function optimally[1]. And thriving workplaces and teams ensure clients get the best services[2]. This is, of course, the end goal for so many organisations. But it should be the ultimate goal of every organisation. And Michelle wanted to see organisations change and drive towards that best outcome for both clients and customers.

Shifting Mindsets

Around 18 years ago, Michelle began to offer training for leaders working in the health industry. Within this training, she integrates the latest research in neuroscience, interpersonal neurobiology, emotional intelligence, and contemporary leadership. Michelle delivers programs in leadership, self-leadership, professional mentoring, workplace wellbeing and professional resilience. She also offers a range of workplace training and facilitation programs in-house. As at the time of printing, Michelle has delivered customised programs to more than 35,000 senior leaders, teams and employees across Australia and New Zealand, in a range of industries.

---

1   World Health Organization & Burton, J. (2010). WHO healthy workplace framework and model: background and supporting literature and practices. World Health Organization. Accessed at https://apps.who.int/iris/handle/10665/113144.

2   WHO. (2010).

Like every consultant, Michelle has her favourite 'baby'. For her, it's the Thriving Professional Women program—a 10-month program focused on the skills working women need to lead themselves to move powerfully and confidently forwards. She loves that the small group size inevitably leads to members developing strong bonds, while the impact and success of past members has also been rewarding.

Michelle has delivered keynotes and presentations at conferences around the world, and her advice has been featured in publications including *Marie Claire* and *GQ Australia*. As a speaker, trainer, facilitator, mentor and author, Michelle is helping to steer workplace ecosystems in a more positive direction, where they can authentically cultivate human potential.

Can an Introvert be Successful in This Space?

One of the biggest challenges for Michelle was being an introvert and, in her own words, a 'very shy person'. She says this created fears around delivering her training programs as well as promoting her practice.

Many of us can no doubt relate when Michelle says she was concerned that delivering training programs often seemed to be the domain of extroverts who were gifted with lots of confidence and humour. 'That is so not me. I'm quite a serious person, quite shy and introverted, a deep thinker and voracious learner. I really wondered whether it was going to be just way too stressful for me, both presenting and promoting my practice.'

She found self-promotion particularly daunting. Michelle knew that to expand her training practice, she would need to work

> *That is so not me. I'm quite a serious person, quite shy and introverted, a deep thinker and voracious learner. I really wondered whether it was going to be just way too stressful for me, both presenting and promoting my practice.*

on marketing and promoting, but she had always viewed it as ego-driven and self-serving, and 'it felt icky and uncomfortable' to her.

Michelle also worried that her sensitive nature would be damaged by the inevitable feedback presenters receive after delivering training programs. 'I just wondered how I would actually manage because I hate disappointing others. I'm a recovering people-pleaser and so I had a lot of fears of putting myself out there. It was easier and felt safer to remain invisible in my counselling practice.'

This is an area many of us struggle with when first deciding to step into our passion. And that's because putting ourselves out there doesn't always come naturally—at least not to all of us. We may engage in a bit of self-sabotage, engaging in activities that hold us back from stepping up and stepping out or believing in self-talk that derails us. I talk about this a lot in my book, *Put Yourself Out There*, and I explore feelings of inadequacy (the imposter syndrome), the scarcity mindset, pity and vanity (where we need constant validation in order to feel good enough to move forward).

The good news is that there are ways to combat those common derailers that stop us from really getting out there and into our passion. Michelle had to do just that in order to step out from the shadows and into her genius zone.

Finding a Starting Point to Empowerment

Like many professionals stepping up to their true calling, Michelle didn't know where to start. When we first started working together, she wasn't sure how to stand in her own expertise and let others know what she had to offer. Fortunately, her passion for her work was a strong enough driving force that it propelled her to find a way forward, no matter how uncomfortable those changes initially were.

'One thing I had on my side was my strong passion for helping workplaces be safe for humans. I was deeply concerned about the negative impact, even trauma, that toxic workplaces were having on good people,' she says.

Together we found ways to instil in Michelle a well-earned confidence in herself and her skills so that she felt ready to expand her practice to where she wanted it to be. Of course, as is always the way with Michelle, she wasn't ready to stop there. She also brought two of her staff to my training. And it was this simple act which helped to empower her team and revolutionise her practice. The team now has ways to talk and think about the positioning and promotion of her practice which has helped it to grow exponentially.

'There are so many brilliant things I gained from Jane's program it's hard to limit it to one,' she says. 'Meeting and working with Jane has been a game-changer to my practice.'

Moving Beyond Fear

When moving into new territory workwise, Michelle is the kind of person who needs to have a framework or scaffolding to help her think strategically, and then act confidently. My Expert to Influencer program was extraordinarily impactful for Michelle. It offered new ways to organise her thoughts and prevent her from getting caught up in her own fears. This gave her the self-confidence to take action and follow the steps needed to move forward in her business.

'The Expert to Influencer program helped me identify and leverage my strengths that could best support my positioning,' she says. 'I focused on using my communication skills and strengths to build relationships in ways that built my positioning. Jane helped demystify the way to build my list, to communicate regularly with my tribe and to start offering free webinars.'

Michelle and her team now have the structure, strategies and confidence in what they are doing—and she says the results have been incredible.

As members of my community will know, it's also imperative to have clarity around your own expertise so you can truly own it and share your wisdom with the world. Michelle participated in my content creation program, which she says 'hit the spot' in a way no other programs had done.

It helped to give Michelle awareness around her own knowledge and expertise, which boosted her confidence and provided a platform for her to move forward. 'It also helped me get unstuck when I was finalising the last two chapters of my book!' she says.

Michelle's book, *Leading Above The Line,* looks at how we can create psychologically aware, responsible and safe workplaces where leaders and employees thrive.

Put to The Test

March 2020 was a month that stands out for many of us, particularly those running a small business. For Michelle it was no different. She was all set to head to New Zealand to deliver training for two weeks when the pandemic hit, and everything changed.

Months of work was suddenly cancelled and she realised she had to adapt to the new context. While at first she had no idea how to achieve this, she did know that people needed support—and that was something she was still able to provide. Michelle ran some free webinars, which were hugely popular and successful, and they gave her the confidence to shift her work online.

Michelle attributes her success in moving her business online to the marketing strategies she learned through my programs. And what a success it was—her practice grew a staggering 60% in the 2021 financial year. She hit milestones that she thought would take years to achieve. And it all came down to empowering herself, and empowering her team.

What Would Michelle Do Differently?

Michelle says that if she had her time again, there are two key things she would do differently. 'The first thing would be to work with Jane from the start. I wasted my time and money on other programs and never found anything that hit the spot for me compared to what I gained through working with Jane,' she says.

Michelle gained a lot of value from understanding what it was to be an 'influencer'. Working with my team helped her to understand how to become an influencer in ways that were not arrogant or egotistical. Michelle saw the value in being visible and consistent. This helped her community understand that she wanted to bring value and support in generous ways.

Michelle found her own strength and confidence to step forward. Previously she had been afraid to stand out from the crowd and didn't value her own wisdom and knowledge. She has now learned that being successful means she can support many others and many workplaces to thrive.

The other thing she would do differently if she had her time again is what she calls 'getting over herself'. She ultimately achieved this by sending out a regular newsletter and running regular webinars, but she wishes she did them far earlier in her business journey.

Continuing to Empower and Optimise

Michelle believes that creating a thriving, high-performing and resilient workforce has never been more vital for organisational success. As businesses grapple with the disruptions caused by the pandemic and start figuring out what their new normal looks like, Michelle says there is a 'once-in-a-lifetime opportunity to realign our working lives, our relationships and our world'. Factors such as employee resilience and mental wellbeing will be vital to building a productive and mindful post-pandemic world.

> *There is a 'once-in-a-lifetime opportunity to realign our working lives, our relationships and our world'.*

In Michelle's view, there has never been a time when the importance of our relationships and the interpersonal climate we collectively create has been more vital to our professional lives and an organisation's success. She will continue to cultivate the best in people and those around them via professional resilience, emotional intelligence, leadership training and mentoring. Having founded Workplace Resilience in 2010, Michelle has since expanded her business and assembled an experienced team to work with organisations who want to improve their productivity by enhancing the interpersonal fabric of the workplace.

Helping people learn how to lead themselves with kindness, more awareness and more respect is a passion of Michelle's. This leads people to greater success, wellbeing and life satisfaction – and of course converts to better results for organisations.

Michelle says her biggest dream is to transform workplaces through supporting self-leadership development. 'I'd love to take these programs to an even wider audience and help organisations transform through better self-leadership. It is truly empowering, and so good for humans and our wellbeing.'

⚷ 3 Key Learnings

1. It doesn't matter if you're shy or introverted – once you see your value and understand the power of your expertise, you can deliver keynotes, lead programs and write books.

2. Being an influencer doesn't mean you have to be arrogant or ego-driven. There are ways you can share your wisdom that feel natural and comfortable.

3. Build your list and communicate regularly with your tribe via newsletters and webinars.

CHAPTER 12

Sharon Francisco

Business Coach to Bookkeepers

BEING YOUR AUTHENTIC SELF

Sharon Francisco—business mentor, accountability coach and motivational hype girl to bookkeepers everywhere—has been such an inspiration to work with. She is truly extraordinary. I adore her authenticity, her energy, her essence and the phenomenal practice she has created. We've known each other for a long time, and I often find myself using her as an example of the value of being yourself, as she has an incredible way of bringing humanness and warmth into her video presentations.

Sharon has had an incredibly successful year. She launched her practice in late 2020 but has already grown from $0 to an impressive $300K revenue. She offers both one-on-one and group coaching to her clients, in addition to her popular program The Entrepreneurial Bookkeeper, which teaches bookkeepers how to scale their business and maximise their success.

But like most triumphs, success didn't happen overnight for Sharon. She says there was much pain and growth on her journey to where she is today.

Seeds of Success

Having grown up in a family of successful entrepreneurs and business owners, Sharon always felt drawn to follow a similar path. In fact, she purchased her first business at the age of 22. After growing and then selling her company, Sharon spent the next 15 years coaching small to medium businesses on the best practices and tactics to grow their business, build great teams and sell with confidence.

In 2013, Sharon joined her sister-in-law in a bookkeeping business, scaling it from $100K with one bookkeeper to more than $700K with 12 bookkeepers. Her success at building a 'black belt' bookkeeping business inspired her to develop The Entrepreneurial Bookkeeper, which shares her formula for success with ambitious number wizards.

Sharon's program covers how to price confidently, how to hire the right team members to ensure they scale their talent and how to fully systemise a business to enjoy the income and freedom that can come with it (when it's done right). Sharon believes it's all about tapping into your fears, delegating the tasks you don't want to do and breaking through your comfort zone.

Sharon's background in sales and business development gave her the knowledge and expertise to coach bookkeepers to skyrocket their businesses. But even her vast expertise didn't stop her from feeling like an imposter. Sharon isn't a bookkeeper or an accountant by trade. In fact, she says numbers are not her forte at all. But what Sharon does specialise in is motivating and working with bookkeepers, because she understands their practices and how they operate. In other words, she gets how they tick. And understanding your customer or client is one of the most important parts of growing a successful business.

Embracing the Real You

In order to get past her imposter feelings, Sharon needed to embrace what she was good at, and understand her own value. Part of her process for doing that was to create her own branding video to explain what she was good at – and not so good at. In fact, it is Sharon's authenticity, standing up in her business branding video admitting that she isn't a bookkeeper or particularly good with numbers, that makes her unique and genuinely compelling to clients. She isn't afraid to be honest and real, which she attributes to her country upbringing where she felt comfortable to be herself.

Sharon says that although her time spent working in the corporate world gave her self-confidence a hit, she soon came back to the real her. 'You go out into the world, and you get knocked around and you go back into yourself, and you think, "Oh OK, now I have to create this version." It shapes you in such a way that you have to become something to survive.' Fortunately, inauthenticity never felt right for Sharon and today she has no problems revealing her true self.

During our time working together, I could see it was this realness that would be Sharon's superpower in working with clients and growing her business. 'You kind of gave me the permission to be me,' she says. 'And I think that was the best gift that anyone could give me because to be yourself is the most liberating, beautiful feeling ever.'

The icing on the cake for Sharon was seeing her clients feel empowered, take on her advice, and then experience success of their own. 'Some of my clients have had some massive wins and successes and it just gives you that reassurance that it's OK to be me and it's going to make a difference. And holy cow, it feels good!'

Making it Happen

I started working with Sharon four or so years ago, but it took her three years before she stepped out and launched The Entrepreneurial Bookkeeper. Even at the very start of our work together, Sharon could feel and see where she wanted to be.

Since she was a little girl, Sharon has known that if someone else can do something, she can too. She looked at what I was doing in my business and knew she could achieve the same for her clients. 'I can take what you're teaching and apply it to my war, and I think that's what I did,' she says. While Sharon always knew she had it in her to achieve great success, it was the boosted self-belief and the tools and the confidence she gained from working together that helped her to really go all in and grab it.

Sharon received a good tax refund one year, which enabled her to take three months off from her full-time job. She used the time to determine what she wanted to achieve and where she wanted to be. 'And I'd say that was one of the most important decisions that I've ever made because I feel like that's when it all came together in my head.'

At the end of the three months, Sharon knew the direction she wanted to take. Things then began lining up for her and doors started opening. She began doing webinars in conjunction with Pure Bookkeeping, an organisation formed to help others finetune the skills needed to run their businesses well. This was the start and the push she needed to start making her work her own.

Running Towards Your Fears

Sharon says she went through a lot of pain to get to the other side of her success, but she was willing to go deep into the fears that came up for her. These fears included not being able to achieve her direction, not having the ability or know-how to grow a practice, not having everything she needed to get started and stepping into her own practice and failing.

Identifying fears is now a fundamental area Sharon works on with her own clients. She encourages them to identify the fears that come up as they think about what they want to achieve in their business. She advises them to go further into those fears and figure out exactly what they are and where they come from in order to move past them. Sharon understands that just like she used to, her clients ran away from their fears because they're not a nice feeling. It's human nature to prefer to go back to our comfort zones, but Sharon doesn't want that to be a barrier to success.

'And whatever that is, it's generally around our self-worth,' she says. 'Whether we think we can do something or not, whatever story you've got—and we know a lot of our stories are not so true sometimes—figure out a story that's going to work for you to get your outcome.'

Sharon says the next step is assembling whatever resources, tools or people you need to help you. For her, working with a mentor and being in Women with Influence was that next step. I could provide her with the tools and resources she needed, particularly around 'think, sell, deliver' which helped her to gain the confidence she needed to take action. 'Confidence is king,' she says.

Trusting the Process

A big thing that I have always really admired about Sharon is that she has always shown up. When we worked together, she would always say, 'OK, I know I'm in the right room and even if I'm feeling uncomfortable, I know I'm in the right space.'

When she first started making her videos, Sharon was unaware they would have such an impact and didn't particularly want to make more. But when I told her they were fantastic, she trusted my experience and worked hard, making almost 40 a day when she didn't feel like making any!

Sharon's trust in the process has been impressive. First she gathered the knowledge and tools, then established her business and applied my methodology—and the results have been incredible. 'I think the analogy is that the elastic band's been stretched back, back, back... and then it's finally been let go, and it's just been phenomenal. Absolutely phenomenal,' she says. 'I think it's the faith that I had in what you taught me.'

It takes a lot to relinquish control and have a go. Sharon is the queen of persistence. She's taken on all the tools and methodologies, but she's worked out her version, her identity and who she is to make that happen. I love that she's trod her own path.

Walking the Talk

It's vital for coaches to be able to walk the talk. We need authenticity—which Sharon has in spades—and accountability to show that we're doing what we're telling our clients to do. Otherwise it's not lived experience and we are simply saying, not doing.

For Sharon, the experience of creating a business that really serves her and doesn't eat up every hour of her day, while still achieving great results for her clients, is a brilliant example to the bookkeepers and accountants who follow her program. Her branding video captures the essence and energy of who she is, and her version of success. As she connects with clients over a cup of coffee and enjoys a personal training session with her friends, she is demonstrating that work/life balance and success can go hand in hand.

> ❝
>
> *Try to identify her target market earlier. 'They are out there, you just have to know where to look and be persistent.*

Sharon hopes to prove to her clients that they can scale their company and do the things they love without feeling like a slave to their business. She has come across many bookkeepers and accountants who are working long hours, and not putting the boundaries in place to preserve their wellbeing. 'They are not generally going to say, no, I can't do this. They'll just keep working and working and working to get the job done, to help the client, to do the right thing by the client... A big part of what I do is to help them to see that they don't need to keep doing that.'

Sharon urges all business owners to be ferocious around protecting and nurturing their mental health by:

- Making mental and physical fitness a priority in your life. Move three to four times a week to raise your heartbeat for 30-45 minutes.

- Eating good, wholesome, simple food and drinking at least two litres of water a day for at least six days a week.

- Being unreasonable with yourself around developing your belief, meaning don't take any of your excuses around what's stopping you. Find the path to unstoppable self-belief the fastest way possible.

Sharon also recommends surrounding yourself with good, wholesome people who believe in you, who have done what you want to do and make you feel fantastic about yourself. Banish all negativity and anything that zaps your energy from your life—whether it's people, things or places.

All About the Timing

If Sharon had her time again, there are a few things she would want to do sooner, such as taking action faster and bringing me on as a coach earlier in the process. She says she would also try to identify her target market earlier. 'They are out there, you just have to know where to look and be persistent,' she says.

Sharon self-sabotaged for several years and wishes she had gone deeper into her fears to resolve them sooner. She would also have done more to boost her self-belief so she could implement my teachings earlier. But at the end of the day, she has reached a phenomenal place, and is giving so much back to her audience simply by embracing her authentic self—all her incredible experience, expertise and even her unconventional background. It all serves to showcase her and her brand.

🔑 3 Key Learnings

1. Take massive action towards the goals you want to achieve. Let setbacks be just that. They are not failures. You've just figured out different ways to not get to your destination. Keep trying.
2. Be prepared to do what others are not and keep going. Don't give up.
3. You have permission to be yourself. There's nothing more liberating than that.

Listen to the Jane Anderson Show Podcast, Episode 56 –
Leadership and Mindset Expert, Sharon Francisco

CHAPTER 13

Belinda Brosnan

Leadership Expert

DRIVEN BY VALUES

Belinda Brosnan is a trusted leadership confidante, change agent, author, speaker and executive coach. Her speciality is navigating uncertainty and helping senior leaders get C-suite ready.

But Belinda wasn't always in the consultant space. In fact, her background was in property development and media. She was compelled to launch her own practice in 2012 after a powerful lightbulb moment that helped her to realise her own personal values – freedom, courage, generosity and the drive to make a difference.

Driven By Values

'I realised that with my values and my strengths, I had a contribution that I could make. It was inevitable that I would work for myself because one of my top values was freedom. And for me, working for myself gave me the freedom to work differently, to be creative and to be able to drive my own destiny.

When I was in a corporate organisation, I felt like I didn't have that control. I felt like I was at the mercy of the bureaucracy, and knew I had more to contribute,' Belinda says.

Initially, Belinda started her business focused on marketing, with a three-year plan to transition into executive coaching and leadership development. But because she was so motivated, she managed to cross that threshold in half the time – an astounding accomplishment.

> ❝
> *I managed to move fully into this space in quite a short amount of time, and I've been happily here for the past 11 years. That was really reaffirming for me.*

'I managed to move fully into this space in quite a short amount of time, and I've been happily here for the past 11 years. That was really reaffirming for me', says Belinda. Through working with a coach, she unlocked her own ability to live her values through her practice.

Now Belinda's practice balances a mix of executive coaching, large-scale leadership development programs within organisations and one-off speaking and workshops. As her practice has evolved, Belinda has become increasingly focused on leading and influencing in these complex and uncertain times. Today she works with large corporate organisations and C-Suite and senior leaders, helping them to navigate uncertainty and change – something that many (if not all) organisations know all too well today.

Belinda credits her own experience in corporate executive roles as one of the unique aspects of her work. She understands what's needed to elevate influence at that level. In fact, one of the key things Belinda has noticed as her practice has evolved is the importance of making a firm commitment to take the reins and lead. She recognises that this is a powerful decision but believes there's no better time than right now to make that decision.

Belinda says, 'Everything about my practice right now is based around powerful decisions that help leaders be influential and adaptive at this time. And with the uncertainty and disruptions in the world, there's been no more important time than now.'

Being Courageous with Change

With a previous life in energetic, busy corporate roles, one of Belinda's challenges was adapting to her new working environment — working from home.

'I had a fear of being isolated because I'd always found that I had my best ideas when I could bounce them off others. I was fearful I would lose that,' explains Belinda. 'I'd always seen myself as quite a straight-to-the-point kind of leader, and suddenly here I was going out on my own.'

Belinda had to cross some big barriers and learn some important lessons in how to work from home and do it well. And one of those lessons was how to connect with people who could help her be the best version of herself.

Many of the consultants in my network have gone through this transition. And since the pandemic, working from home and operating solo has impacted more and more people even beyond the consulting or freelancing space.

Like many who have suddenly found themselves in this situation, Belinda began to question herself. She wondered, 'How can I do my best work in these new conditions? How can I unlock my ideas?' She needed the home-based equivalent of work colleagues with whom she could collaborate, bounce ideas and stretch her own experiences and understanding. Eventually she would find them but, in the meantime, she learned to love working from home. It was an adaptation that many of the women in our network have had to make. Like them, Belinda learned to embrace the benefits of being a solo operator, and her business began to grow.

The Freedom to Make Mistakes... and Learn from Them

With her practice doing well, including signing a large contract, Belinda took a big step by employing someone to work with her. But it perhaps wasn't the right time.

Belinda says, 'I made that classic business mistake in the early days of getting so caught up in the work, thinking that it was all locked and loaded, that I began employing people. And then I had a big contract pulled and suddenly I was left thinking, "Holy crap! How do I fill the income bucket now?"'

Belinda realised that she needed to review what was essential for her business operations. And although it was challenging when that contract was pulled, it made her begin to examine how to make her business sustainable in the long term. This analysis highlighted two major stumbling blocks.

The first and primary stumbling block was that Belinda needed a mentor. Although she was (and is) an organised person, she wasn't structured. A mentor would help Belinda focus within her business. Secondly, she needed to get certain foundational elements in place that would allow her to excel in the aspects of her work at which she thrived.

> *I would say we have a very strong shared value in making a difference through generosity. Jane takes the cake on generosity, and that's been very much an important part of our relationship.*

Creating Connections

Belinda says, 'When I connected with Jane, we really bonded over our similar marketing backgrounds and the fact that we were both Queenslanders and originally regional girls too. Also, both of us are very driven to make a difference in the work that we do.'

'I would say we have a very strong shared value in making a difference through generosity. Jane takes the cake on generosity, and that's been very much an important part of our relationship,' Belinda shares.

The Ability to be Generous with Herself

Now that Belinda had found my team and her values-based purpose, her work life was going very well. But as we all know, life doesn't stop even when we're working hard on our business. And when Belinda's friend was diagnosed with incurable cancer, she found herself dealing with one of life's most challenging moments. She had to make some decisions on how to continue to keep her business running and thriving while also creating space to deal with a personal crisis.

Belinda says, 'That was a really fearful time for me. I felt incredibly alone, and started to have some doubts, in terms of my abilities. I felt that I was being pulled in all directions, taking on too many opinions from people who were experts – who, although amazing at what they did — didn't have the insight into my world at that time,' says Belinda.

The timing was challenging. Having just written her book, Start with You: Lead from the Inside, Belinda was moving into a period where she really should have been pushing her business, and her book, out into the world. But she was held back by a focus that was too fractured as she wanted to spend more time with her friend. Belinda realised that she couldn't go as full throttle as she wanted to and made the decision to pull back for a while.

COVID hit just as Belinda's friend passed away and created a very challenging situation. But when Belinda was ready to get back into her business, her business was ready for her. She explains, 'The best thing that I implemented from working with Jane, is her systematic approach to things. As someone who likes to be creative, I can sometimes lack structure, and I don't always have the tools or systems in place that I need.'

Belinda and I worked together to implement systems that gave her the structure and tools her practice needed as it gained traction again. Belinda found that she tended to overestimate what she could get done in a particular time, and sometimes that meant important stuff was missed. I reiterated how essential systems are to our practice, and how important it is to have those different things in place. They really can help us be at the cutting edge for our clients.

After working together, Belinda saw that having structure around the way she worked created freedom. And implementing the foundational things into her approach to work helped to increase her productivity and focus. Just as Belinda had experienced, in life one never knows what's waiting around the corner – maybe it's an illness, a family problem, a lost contract or a missed deadline. Having a structure in place helped to elevate Belinda's business. It will also provide a cushion for the next challenge that she faces.

Fresh Eyes

Belinda understands the power of having a fresh pair of eyes, new insight and a different perspective. She believes this has been hugely impactful for her business. 'I think the thing Jane has brought me is a deep knowledge of the impact that I can have. She helps me cut through the weeds and see what's really there from a big picture perspective.'

'I think Jane is a true trend setter, and her acknowledgement of the fact that we need to be futurist in our business has been reinforced for me.' Belinda believes that we always need to be looking to the future and thinking about things in new ways to ensure that we aren't left behind.

Trusting Your Gut and Backing Yourself

Belinda has taken all her experience, skills and insights and implemented them into her practice with outstanding results. But of course, there are things she wished she'd done differently. In particular she wishes that she'd be more circumspect about who she took advice from in the beginning. She says, 'I wouldn't necessarily seek out the advice of every single person around me before making some key decisions. Instead, I'd back my gut and instinct more.'

Trusting your gut and backing yourself is an important part of succeeding as a consultant, because you don't necessarily have anyone else backing you. You need to trust yourself and trust your decisions. And for Belinda she's learned to trust not just her decision-making processes, but also the profitability of the programs that she runs. It's about being realistic in business and reviewing your offerings.

She says, 'If a program isn't working, and you've tweaked it a couple of ways, and it's still not working, then sometimes it's time to cut that baby loose.' Again, it's about trusting what is right for your business.

Making a Difference

As a leading change agent on mindset and personal leadership through challenge and uncertainty, Belinda is obsessed with practical solutions for her clients. She is passionate about reinventing the patterns of thinking and behaviour that hold people back from being effective collaborators, leaders and decision makers. But at the heart of Belinda's practice is her intention to make a difference and have an impact, particularly in making wise decisions.

'When everything feels uncertain is when the temptation to be reactive shows itself. We tend to make decisions that get in the way of where we really want to head.' She aims to create more impact in her work by getting her message out to more people. 'We are experiencing a revolution in how we work and connect with one another, and there is a new leadership intelligence now required for thriving,' says Belinda.

Belinda wants to see less anxiety, less overwhelm and more people trusting themselves to take risks — and feeling secure in the fact that they have systems in place that can make that happen. 'So, for me, that is a big dream that I have. I think there's a heavy weight on the shoulders of the world right now, and I'd like to lift it a little. I know I can make a massive difference.'

🔑 3 Key Learnings

1. Get Specific. One of the biggest challenges Belinda had in the early years of her practice was the distraction of different ideas, different systems, different tools and different opinions. By being specific on the things she needed at different times she gained the freedom to make the progress she needed in her business.
2. Get Connected. Belinda emphasises that you don't need to go it alone – you need support. Having the benefit of different perspectives and the belief in yourself to come back to the core of what's most important to you, makes that support invaluable.
3. Get Systems. Belinda is a true believer in systems and processes. She is a true believer in the foundational support they can bring to a business to help see her (and anyone) through challenging times.

CHAPTER 14

Joanne Love

High Performance Expert

ACHIEVING YOUR GOALS

Helping people to realise their potential is Joanne Love's purpose. She is a high-performance expert, a keynote speaker and has worked with clients in education, business, the sporting world and the everyday world. But for Joanne, it all began in the Olympic arena.

Joanne was a successful Olympic-medal-winning coach who worked with many high-performance athletes in Australia and internationally. While she loved coaching, it was the emotional and mental aspects that really interested her. Ultimately, Joanne's experience helping athletes to set effective goals to increase emotional wellbeing led her to study psychology at university.

With this degree in her pocket, Joanne added to her wealth of knowledge and her high-performance skillset. So she stepped out of the sporting arena to work directly with corporate clients, helping them to set goals and take the small steps needed to achieve big results.

Building resilience through effective goal setting and implementation strategies is something we can all benefit from, in our personal and business lives. We all get knocked down. We sometimes need help getting back up again, staying on track and safeguarding our wellbeing. Joanne's 25 years of experience as a high-performance expert means she knows what it takes to succeed and achieve, in any environment. And that's just what she helps her clients to do.

Olympic Beginnings

Like so many truly awe-inspiring stories, Joanne's began in the Olympic arena. She was a swimming coach and represented Australia at the Beijing 2008 Olympics. During this competition, one of her athletes experienced failure. Like it would for many of us, failure had a big impact on the athlete's overall wellbeing.

Joanne struggled to understand how to best help her athlete. She wanted to learn more so she could help more, as helping people realise their potential is Joanne's purpose. And it was this driver that sent her back to university to study psychology.

Joanne soon realised that what can be applied in elite sport can be applied every day for every one of us. Really, when it comes down to it, our problems are universal. Whether it's stepping up to the block to start a race or standing up to speak in a meeting, we can set goals to improve our performance while safeguarding our wellbeing.

A Stumbling Block

When Joanne stepped out of the world she knew, helping athletes and coaches realise their potential, she faced her own stumbling block. 'Learning how to sell myself to other people, learning how to tell my story and learning how to help other people was a whole education itself,' Joanne says. She wishes she'd taken the time to plan her brand within her practice from the very beginning.

As she progressed in her work, Joanne realised she needed a lot more brand name recognition to take the next step and grow her business. And it was all part and parcel of learning to sell herself in a way that felt natural and in tune for her.

This is where working with our community has really helped Joanne. For many of the consultants and practitioners within our network, incorporating their personal brand into messaging and programs is not something that comes naturally. But there comes a time when it's essential to reach the next level of engagement for your business.

It All Starts with Why

When Joanne expanded her client base from athletes, she noticed that a common stumbling block to people achieving their goals was understanding why they want something. 'A lot of people go into it wanting to achieve certain things, but they don't understand why they want it,' she says. Whether that's wanting a particular car, or house or increasing their annual revenue, it all comes back to why they want that particular thing.

Joanne credits the work of Simon Sinek when she says it's essential to understand the 'why' behind your goals[1]. His work suggests that your 'why' must align with the goal, for the goal to be effective and achievable.

Know Your Purpose

When we're building a brand, we don't always think about our purpose – the compelling reason why what you have to say matters. Joanne says that knowing your purpose (your 'why') is essential to setting effective goals. But more importantly, it's also vital to your wellbeing. Whether your goal is to increase revenue, engage more clients or be a keynote speaker, you must be clear on your reasons why.

Joanne says that 'when a goal has a purpose behind it, it helps you to stay mentally well' and on track. A perfect example is when someone has experienced a lot of adversity and hit rock bottom. It's like a big wakeup call. They'll often find themselves asking, 'what's my purpose in life?' In this situation, it's human nature to start thinking about what really matters and what you really

> ❝
> *When a goal has a purpose behind it, it helps you to stay mentally well.*

---

1   Sinek, S. 'Our WHY: To inspire people to do the things that inspire them so that, together, each of us can change our world for the better.' Accessed at https://simonsinek.com/our-why/.

want. And it's from there that you can start to plan and implement it. If you know your purpose, it will help in setting your goals and achieving them.

Know Your Values

Knowing your purpose, the reason you get up each morning, is the first step. But the second step is understanding how your purpose aligns with your values. Ask yourself, 'what do you stand for?' A goal to make a million dollars is one thing – but why is that your goal? Is a million dollars alone going to make you happy in life, or would you like to be happy with less? In Joanne's experience, when people have a perpetual drive to buy a better car or a better house, they are not necessarily any happier. In fact, they can often be more miserable.

What makes us 'happy' or content with life is up to each of us. If we are clear as to our purpose and it is in tune with our personal values, Joanne tells us that that's when we will succeed, be at our happiest and be the most content with life. That is when our mental wellbeing will be at its best.

Be In Control

Joanne spoke at one of our events on the Gold Coast a couple of years ago, and something she said really resonated with me. She was talking about Olympic gold medals versus times. In the high-performance sporting world, setting a goal to win only sets you up for failure and creates unbelievable expectations and pressure.

Joanne says that 'goals should never be set towards winning'. After all you can't control how fast someone else may run or how much money someone else may make. She says, 'You must be in control of your goals because you can't control how others may perform. But you can control the time that you want to do, or some part of your performance that you want to do. So, the best goals are the ones that allow you to be totally in control of what you're doing.'

This is a fascinating insight into what Joanne has learned and experienced – to not have a goal that chases something elusive or comparative but instead focuses on your own individual progress and improvement.

Contain Your Ego

Setting goals that compare yourself to someone or are achieved when you become better than a competitor can unleash your ego. And as Joanne says, 'our ego can be our worst enemy'. If we set unrealistic goals based on winning alone, and then underestimate the effort and skill required to achieve them, it can lead to self-sabotage. And that leads us to making excuses for why we can't do certain things. Joanne says we must control our ego and what we *can* do to the best of our ability and stay in control.

Setting Effective Goals

Today's Joanne's expertise is focused on knowing how to set effective goals so we can achieve our dreams. Joanne helps people to set effective goals, which incorporate purpose (their 'why'), their values, and a well-defined strategy to get there. This provides 'a beautiful map for the motivation and momentum to keep us going,' she says.

Creating a constant pattern of smaller goals, along the way to bigger goals, is crucial. Joanne says we should set two smaller goals that we can achieve and one that will push us to stretch. This 'stretch-goal' should be one that we absolutely believe in, but that could make others laugh in disbelief.

Setting small goals to achieve daily, weekly, monthly, three monthly, six monthly and yearly outcomes, will create your constant pattern of goals. They must be realistic and achievable, while you challenge yourself to work towards your stretch-goal. 'When we've got a goal that scares us, it makes us work towards it,' Joanne says. Achieving the smaller goals along the way rewards us with boosts of dopamine, which push us on to the next goal.

Joanne says there's a consensus in the medical world that we are all low in dopamine, which can put us at risk of depression as well as Parkinson's disease. If we set lots of small goals and reward ourselves regularly with a dopamine boost, we can safeguard our mental health as we continue to work towards our stretch-goals.

Reaching Her Target Audience

Despite her incredible knowledge, experience, and expertise, at one point on her journey Joanne was struggling to convey her own values to her potential clients. She had everything she needed to create an excellent experience and give them incredible value – but she didn't have the methodology to succinctly present it. And she was missing out on opportunities because of it.

We worked together to nail down what her value is. What she offers her clients, and the outcomes they can expect. We pulled together a white paper that allowed her to have something in hand for sales meetings that would demonstrate what she did and why it benefits each client. This cut-through all the rigamarole that she was going through previously as she attempted to convey her value and made it clear and upfront.

This was the step she needed to stop struggling through sales meetings... and she's never looked back!

Plan to Fail

As an elite coach, and a practitioner with her own business, Joanne understands what it means to fail (as we all do). But she also believes that we should accept and plan to fail along the way to achieving our goals. Many of us in the consulting space are working by ourselves, and so building resilience into our plans is essential to keeping the momentum going. We need to be clear about what our goals are and how we will achieve them. We need to be our own cheerleader to get back on track if we stumble.

Failure is a part of life. But when we've set effective goals, we are more resilient and don't fall in a heap when we meet an obstacle. Of course, planning is key for this. It helps us understand what we're looking to achieve. Then, when we meet obstacles, we can work through them, building resilience and wellbeing along the way.

Words of Wisdom

Joanne's advice for anyone growing their practice is to reach out for guidance as early as you can. It can be very hard when you don't know how or what to do with your personal brand or any other element of your business, particularly when you are already busy working to keep all the balls in the air.

Joanne suggests that the best approach is to simply keep moving forward, setting goals and planning to achieve them. This is so you don't have to pause and backward-plan each time you are ready to take the next step. Joanne says that 'if I had my time again, I would work more on that', learning what to do in the personal branding space, so her brand name recognition is in place, ready to take each next step.

3 Key Learnings

1. Align the purpose and values behind your goals.
2. Set effective goals; two small goals along the way to a stretch-goal. Write them down.
3. Plan to fail, so obstacles don't derail your momentum and knock you off track.

Listen to the Jane Anderson Show Podcast, Episode 48, High-Performance Expert, Joanne Love

CHAPTER 15

Emma McQueen

Business Coach to Female Entrepreneurs

MASTERFUL SELF-STARTER

This business coach, director, author, podcaster, speaker and mum of three girls is an all-round legend. In fact, when Emma McQueen enters a room with her go-getter energy, she commands attention.

Having worked for more than 20 years across recruitment, human resources and leadership development, Emma now focuses on the niche that truly fills her professional and personal cup – cheering on women in business. She is their ultimate cheerleader, sharing her signature firm-but-fair feedback and motivating them to kick career goals and exceed their own expectations. Emma knows that success and happiness in business flows on to everything in life, and that life is too short to be unhappy or disengaged at work.

We love having Emma as part of our Exceptional Women community. She joined our community in its early days and has since helped me behind the scenes with phenomenally successful events like the COVID-19-inspired Content Creation Bootcamps.

From Side Hustle to Centre Stage

Emma's passion for business coaching first came to life as a sideline gig. At the time she was working full-time in HR and leadership development for World Vision Australia. She joined Women & Leadership Australia (WLA), where she helped facilitate personal growth and progression for some of the nation's top female executives. At any given point, Emma could be responsible for coaching a cohort of up to 35 women. As a masterful self-starter with a strong entrepreneurial drive, Emma thrived on the adrenaline. It drove her to be better, more efficient and more proficient.

But it wasn't until her safe and comfortable job was tested and structural changes rippled through the company that Emma took a leap of faith and turned her side hustle into her primary career. When she came home one night and confided in her husband that she didn't particularly want any of the new positions within the company, and maybe she would find another HR director position with a different brand, it was her husband who changed her thinking.

'He just looked at me and said, "For five years, I've heard you bang on about having your own business. Don't you think it's time?" And I'm like, "Yes, it is time. Thank you very much!"'

It's a little ironic that Emma's decision to be a career cheerleader for so many other women hinged upon the moment where she herself needed a cheerleader. She admits that if it wasn't for her husband spurring her on, she may never have launched her business and found the work that genuinely lights her up.

Finding Her Niche

Emma has been working in her business full-time for about five years. Over that period, she's tested the waters in a number of different areas but has now found that thing we're all ultimately searching for in our careers – the beautiful sweet-spot where talent and desire intersect. But for Emma, her professional strengths are so well aligned with her passions that there's no doubt that her work is her true calling.

While Emma also offers her business and corporate success coaching services to men, it is women who really drive her purpose. She loves being the one to help female entrepreneurs fall back in love with their work or move on to new challenges that help them tap into their potential. At the end of the day, we all deserve to be fulfilled and excited by our work, right?

Like anything worth fighting for, it took Emma a little time and research to find her niche. One of her most popular coaching programs, Thriving Women, was developed as a result of many clarity calls with potential female clients. One of the strong themes coming up in these preliminary chats was the loneliness women often felt in business. These stories resonated with Emma, and her own experiences helped her to get really clear on exactly who her audience was and what they needed. She knew that by facilitating a group setting she could not only help her clients get the results they wanted in a coaching environment but also help build a strong, safe community around them. The 12-month program is now in its fourth year and has evolved over time to make it the successful platform it is today.

The Importance of Systems

While you may stalk Emma's Instagram and think her workdays are all rainbow roller skates and strawberry teacups, she is the first to admit it's not always as fun and breezy as it looks. She says that while there are some periods when everything hums along beautifully and easily, it never lasts. The key, according to Emma, is in the preparation. 'I think it starts to look effortless when you've got good systems in place,' she says.

After a very successful – and very busy – first year in business, Emma quickly realised that in order to keep afloat she would have to systemise. As many of those in our community and in the business world know, in the early days of growing a business you'll probably say yes to just about every opportunity thrown your way. Emma agrees that when you're starting out it's important to try a few things, work out what's in your wheelhouse, what you're passionate about and if you can make money from it. And so, she spent her first year flat out building her brand and showing up to everything in an effort to build her profile.

But again, it took a few wise words from her husband for the lightbulb to go off. He said, 'You've had an amazing year, but really, is it sustainable?' And so, Emma started to get more clarity around what the core of her work was and who she wanted to serve.

Knowing When to Say No

Emma says that because her background was in HR, she often got pulled into HR work for her clients, which no longer lit her up. When she first started out in coaching, she also did a lot of mediation, which she didn't enjoy at all. It took a while to build the clarity around who exactly she wanted to serve, and to eventually start saying no to those she didn't. Now she has the confidence to respectfully say no to potential clients when they don't align, particularly those from the corporate world.

'We got really deliberate about actually who our target market is. And that is women who have their own business, normally a service-based business, or women who are in leadership roles and working one-on-one with them.' When someone isn't a great fit, she always ensures she is honest and transparent in a follow-up email or phone call. By explaining that they're not in alignment and instead providing a list of recommendations of other coaches that might be better suited, Emma aims to display professionalism and build trust.

Last year, she went so far as to decide that she would no longer do any training and development programs in the corporate space. 'We're actively saying no to corporate gigs now, which is lovely. It's lovely to be able to be in that position to make that choice', she says. Of course, it has taken a lot of hard work and growth to get to that position, but this clear vision helps Emma stay on track doing the work where her passion and purpose meet.

Exceptional Discipline

One of the things that makes Emma truly exceptional is her gift of discipline. I think if we could all have a tenth of the discipline that Emma has, this country's productivity would go through the roof!

Emma is always consistent in doing the work and showing up in her business. When she decided she wanted to write a book, she was feeling insecure about her writing skills – so she spent the next two years writing a regular newsletter to build up her skills and confidence. After two years, she had convinced herself that yes, in fact, she did have something valuable to contribute.

Her next step was spending a couple of days in my program, working the book out and leveraging off her white paper and newsletter content. By the time our program ended she hadn't entirely completed the book, so off she went to her hotel room and made herself a deal – she wouldn't order her pizza reward until she had completely finished. The result was Emma's fantastic book, *Go-getter: Raise your mojo, shift your mindset and thrive*, which ties into her Thriving Women program.

> ❝
>
> *If we could all have a tenth of the discipline that Emma has, this country's productivity would go through the roof.*

Emma also knew that using a traditional publisher for her book would mean that all of the buyers' information would go to that company and she wouldn't be any wiser about who her readers were. So instead, she used BookPOD to self-publish and was able to follow up directly with people who bought her book, helping to build up her community and network. Having a book has also helped her to position herself as an expert in the space, as well as efficiently share who she is with potential clients before they start working together.

The same has held true for the audio version of her book and her podcast, *Tea with the Queen*. In her podcast, Emma chats with a range of female leaders and businesswomen to share their stories and talk success, failure and fulfilment.

Building Your List

Emma has been fantastic at implementing much of the advice coming out of my Expert to Influencer Masterclass. Her consistency in delivering her podcasts and newsletters has been amazing, and she understands the importance of building her list but does it in such a way that it feels natural and genuine. Yet again, she is ever the masterful self-starter.

> 66
>
> *The discipline of building your list rain, hail or shine may not be sexy, but it's important and it needs to happen every day.*

I find that many people, particularly women, are scared of building a list. So, for those who need to build their list but are hesitant in doing so – you can certainly take notes from the 'Queen'.

Emma admits that at first she found it hard to wrap her head around the idea of building her list. She got lost in the details and over-thinking how she could build numbers and what she could offer. But she soon realised that she had to take a step back. Offering something of value or having an event like her Business with the Queen networking sessions, is a very elegant and subtle way of building your list.

Even now, five years on, Emma remains focused on building her list. 'It never stops because people evolve, people change, people drop off, people come on, but you've got to keep building your list', she says. The discipline of building your list rain, hail or shine may not be sexy, but it's important and it needs to happen every day.

The Power of the Quadrants = Exceptional Positioning

Emma believes that our four Expert to Influencer Quadrants (Educate, Awareness, Network, Direct Contact) are what helped her to achieve such fantastic positioning over the last five years. She went from people not having a clue who she was to people being surprised and delighted when she called. That is the power of positioning. 'It's the power of the quadrants, right? Making sure that you're spending quality time in each of the quadrants and making sure that you're actually just getting the work done without the excuses, without the rigmarole, simply and quickly and with discipline,' she says.

Emma is the poster child for implementing each of the quadrants we talk about in the methodology. For Educate, she's producing podcasts and generating other content. For Awareness, Emma runs Business with the Queen networking events, her Instagram page and general outreach activities. For Network (or Search), she works on thanking her referral partners and has invested in her SEO and LinkedIn strategy. For Direct Contact, Emma makes sales calls each day and distributes her newsletter each week.

Emma has every aspect of the model ticked and makes great choices about how she can develop her own version of it and make it work for her. As a busy mum of three, she has limited time and has to work out where she is going to invest her time to get the biggest bang for her buck.

What's Next

Emma is in a powerful position in her own business now, and as an exceptional woman in business, is someone that we could all learn from. She has a wonderful knack for cheering others on and a refreshing, tough-love approach. She has the rare ability to take the awkwardness out of networking events and is one of those wonderful women who loves to see others in the sisterhood shine.

I have no doubt that Emma will continue kicking goals and levelling up her business. She has achieved such great clarity over the past few years – she knows exactly what she does and who she works with and stays true to that vision. Her goal now is to create a bigger impact in her work.

Emma is now able to help others. She works pro bono with young female entrepreneurs aged around 15 to 16 who are starting their businesses and need some guidance. This has long been a vision of hers but she knew she had to get the foundations and systems in her own business in place before she could help others.

Combining her passion, her purpose and her work – Emma is truly an exceptional self-starter!

🔑 3 Key Learnings

1. Practise discipline. Take a leaf out of Emma's book and bring more discipline and consistency to growing your business. Whether it's ensuring your newsletter always goes out on time or staying committed to building your list, every small act combines to make a big difference to the success of your company over the long term.

2. Building your list doesn't have to feel awkward. Try to think of different ways you can build your list without being too obvious. Offer something of value or invite people to an event.

3. Pay attention to the Quadrants. Emma believes that the power of the Quadrants can help achieve great positioning. If you want to be seen as a leader in your industry, focus on consistently implementing each of the Quadrants.

Listen to the Jane Anderson Show Podcast, Episode 67, Director, Author, Leadership & Business Coach, Emma McQueen

CHAPTER 16

Jessica Schubert

Leadership and Future of Work Expert

CLARITY & CONFIDENCE

Jessica Schubert has worked in many different industries across different continents. At the core of her varied work is a curiosity and desire for connection with people. It's this deep caring that has permeated her careers in hospitality, education, real estate and now coaching.

Given Jessica's background, it's no surprise that today she leads a global leadership practice supporting people around the world to realise their potential, be happier, more confident and more resilient. As the founder and executive coach of Intact Teams, Jessica helps individuals and teams to be the best they can.

Global Beginnings Leads to a Fortuitous Fluke

Jessica's unique accent usually prompts people to ask where she's from. Born and raised in Germany, she has since worked in six different countries, including New Zealand, Hong Kong, Japan and Australia. Today, she calls Melbourne home.

While working for a real estate company in Hong Kong in 2013, Jessica was developing and leading large cross-cultural teams across Asia. Over time in this role, she realised she needed extra tools to help her salespeople unlock and grow into their true potential. She took a coaching course to learn how to help people overcome challenges and develop leaders.

On the first day of the coaching course, Jessica almost gave up. She didn't think it was for her. But by day three, Jessica had decided coaching was what she wanted to do with the rest of her life. This was a huge shift and one that led her to where she is today.

Slowly Building Up The Business

Following her new purpose didn't happen overnight. It was a slow burn for Jessica, who gradually built up her side gig in coaching while decreasing the time spent working in her former full-time job. She practised on colleagues and teams before gaining referrals from strangers. Soon enough, Jessica registered her coaching business and started charging her clients. She reduced her full-time job to part-time, then to contract work. She also worked as an associate for other leadership companies, which she wholeheartedly recommends as it gave her experience in facilitating workshops and different coaching practices.

COVID-19 was the catalyst to finally take a leap of faith. Jessica quit her contracting work and began to focus full time on her leadership practice, Intact Teams. Being based in Melbourne during the period of lockdowns proved to be a difficult time to be running a leadership practice – particularly when many of her would-be-clients were also dealing with lockdowns and the associated economic and physical difficulties.

Fortunately, Jessica is an optimist and knew she could rise to the challenge. She used the time well and started writing her first book, *Lead the Future*. The book touches on what I think is Jessica's mastery, and what makes her exceptional – her relationships with people. She has built and maintained such great connections to so many people in so many different countries over the years.

Jessica's business has been on an impressive trajectory over the last few years, particularly launching full-time just as COVID-19 hit. Intact Teams works with both individuals and groups to help realise their full potential. The key focus is on running transformational programs for a cohort, group or team, supporting them to make the transformation from where they are now to where they need to be.

Jessica says that while the foundational skills of leadership haven't changed much, the landscape we find ourselves in has changed extraordinarily. Intact Teams helps leaders step up and boost their leadership skills, as well as adopt the new leadership skills that are required by industry and community to truly lead the future.

An Exceptional Woman With Influence

Jessica came to one of our Women With Influence dinners in her adopted home of Melbourne and it's been incredibly rewarding watching her journey of growth since that time. She has been able to successfully drive her practice the way that she wanted to – writing her book, working on her positioning and growing her thought leadership. She is incredibly consistent with sending out her newsletters, maintaining her social media, educating the market, being interviewed on podcasts, and also working on rolling out some great programs. Jessica juggles it all and makes it look so easy, but I know that behind the scenes, a lot of hard work goes on.

Learning to Scale

Jessica says that before she joined our Women With Influence community, she had been feeling lost in her coaching practice. While she worked incredibly well with her clients and developed strong, loyal connections with them, she couldn't find a way to scale her business. Instead, she tried out too many things and became sidetracked. 'I tried to be everything for everyone,' she says.

This isn't the first time that I've seen exceptional women bogged down by the little things while trying to grow into their big picture. It's the messy middle of business growth and it's here that many thought leaders and consultants need support.

> *When we talk about positioning, it's not just about* what *you* know, *but it's about what you're passionate about and where you can add the most value.*

We helped Jessica get back on track and get really clear on her offering and positioning. And when we talk about positioning, it's not just about *what* you know, but it's about what you're passionate about and where you can add the most value. We showed her how to stay true to her strengths and focus on the clients she could give the most value to and who she most wanted to work with herself. For Jessica, that was B2B organisations.

Jessica took on all the information and learnings and ran with it. One of the things that makes Jessica so exceptional is that she's a 'just get on with it' person. Coming from large companies with their own in-house marketing teams, there were many tasks she'd never had to do before – but she took on every suggestion with a smile and simply worked at it until she'd ticked it off the list. Before working with us, Jessica had never sent out a newsletter or put an email marketing system in place. She quickly learned how to get the ideas out of her head and contact her list with the right content at the right time.

> **For Jessica, her practice is at the point now where it is more focused on positioning, rather than just activity.**

Jessica is a truly exceptional communicator and relationship builder. This has been a great advantage for building her list and inviting people into her world. She shares content, posts on social media – and wrote her book – in her own unique way. Jessica can choose which individual tasks work for her and Intact Teams and puts them to excellent use in her communications, marketing, and sales. Being a global practice means she must also offer content that's accessible for people all over the world, in different time zones.

From Action to Positioning

Jessica says the first two years of running her leadership practice full-time was focused on activity. She ran Facebook Lives, published webcasts and hosted breakfasts between lockdowns. She was a member of different communities where she spoke and ran masterclasses.

Now that her practice is busy, with many delivery commitments, Jessica spends a significant amount of time working with clients. It's become increasingly difficult to keep up the cadence of business development. She says that the activities her practice focuses on have had to change. For many of us at this stage of business, we might not have time to do lots of activity (such as webcasts), but we can still focus on positioning such as SEO, posting and asking for referrals. For Jessica, her practice is at the point now where it is more focused on positioning, rather than just activity.

Staying In Your Genius

In the early days of visualising her future leadership practice, Jessica imagined an office full of employees. But after several discussions together, she moved away from that idea and is far happier with her reality today, which is a lean, global business.

That's not to say she doesn't have support. This was another topic we discussed during coaching. Jessica decided she needed support in managing a few tasks that were no longer worth spending her own time on, such as social media systems, calendar management and bookkeeping. This helped her to stay in her true genius.

Jessica realised she needed to keep coming up with her thought leadership and intellectual property and developing her great ideas. Getting support for her systems and tasks enabled Jessica to focus on and stay in her true genius. So that's what she did!

Stop Comparing Yourself to Others

Comparing yourself to others and getting distracted by what others are doing in business is a very common challenge to overcome. Jessica says that she wishes she didn't get so sidetracked early on.

'I think one of the challenges that I've had – and I see other people have, in particular women who start running their own practices – is that we tend to look at other people and what they do, and we get this fright of, "Oh my god, they're amazing. They're running a practice that's much larger. Their IP looks amazing. They've got all of this stuff done and they're driving a certain revenue."' This comparison mindset can leave you feeling frozen in place, feeling that you'll never catch up so why bother trying.

Fortunately, Jessica found a sense of kinship in our community and was able to learn from and be inspired by others – rather than comparing herself and her practice to them. Everyone is at different stages within our community, and so members can share and learn from each other without judgement or comparison.

Clarity and Confidence

Jessica's advice for anyone early on in their business journey is to believe that you add value. You can do that by focusing on what you're good at and what your purpose is. She suggests getting really clear on who you are, what your strengths are and what your coaching practice stands for.

'We all know that if you want people to trust you and buy from you or get you in, they need to know who you are, and you have to be able to tell them what you bring to the table,' she says. It's all about having the mindset that you're already adding value. She also believes it's important to be brave and have big dreams.

> **"**
> *It's all about having the mindset that you're already adding value.*

Finally, Jessica sees the key as focusing on three key things you want to do really well. 'That's what I did. I knew that I needed to increase my list, I needed to be able to get in touch with people and stay in touch with them.' This is a great way to narrow down that overwhelming, never-ending to-do list when you're starting out in your business.

Jessica has done so much work mastering the foundations of her business, and now her practice is flourishing. She is so well respected as a coach and is really leading the way and setting the standard in that space. That exceptionality that we talk about is about finding what it is that makes you different – so valuing your uniqueness – and being able to say, 'Well, this is what I bring to the table'. This gets people in the door and wanting to work with you. And from there, it's all about improving.

🔑 3 Key Learnings

1. Just start. When Jessica first joined the Women with Influence community, she didn't even have a newsletter system in place. But she didn't give excuses or find reasons not to do tasks – she just took the advice and started.

2. Narrow your focus. Think about three things that are going to really help grow your practice, and then show up consistently.

3. Change your mindset. Know that you are already adding value right now. You need the confidence in your abilities and the clarity around what you bring to be able to grow your business.

Listen to the Jane Anderson Show Podcast, Episode 68, Leadership Coach, Change Expert, Facilitator & Founder of Intact Teams, Jessica Schubert

CHAPTER 17

WHERE TO FROM HERE

For women in consulting, this book covers a lot of ground. From what you need to really grow your practice, to what might hold you back or derail you. Growing your consulting practice might be one of the toughest things you'll ever do. But as we can see from the exceptional women featured here, it can certainly be done.

The concepts in the book are designed to start the conversation and inspire you rather than make you feel overwhelmed. I've brought these women together to be an inspiration to other women in consulting, and to consider how you might build your brand, trust and influence in similar ways. The featured women demonstrate how they faced down and overcame their own challenges to build successful practices that are thriving.

The ideas behind this book and the platform are designed to help give you a framework to consider, measure and gain insights into the areas where you have strengths and other areas that are an opportunity to focus on and improve. The key is to take control of your own practice, wherever you are today, and begin the process of building and growing. You might be in a position where you're still facing initial challenges. You may be in the position of having had some setbacks, or you may be in a time where you are truly growing and thriving.

Wherever you are, these messages are here for you.

I would love to hear how you go implementing these tactics for growth and success within your own practice. Please reach out to share your stories and examples to me at **jane@jane-anderson.com.au**.

I'm cheering you on!

WORK WITH JANE

In a world of constant change, there is a greater need for consultants and experts in their field to lead and help their clients navigate change. To do this they need a highly influential personal brand, catalyst content and effective business support to build their tribe.

With over 25 years' experience and named as one of the top three branding experts in the world, Jane has helped over 100,000 people to build their identity and influence. She is a certified speaker, coach and has been featured on *Sky Business*, *The Today Show*, *The Age*, *Sydney Morning Herald*, *BBC* and *Management Today*. The author of nine books, Jane typically speaks at conferences, runs workshops, consults, and coaches and focuses especially on female leaders, helping them to build their personal brand, thought leadership and sales.

Jane holds one of the top 1% viewed LinkedIn profiles and is the host of the Jane Anderson Show Podcast where she has interviewed modern thinkers such as Seth Godin.

Jane has been nominated for and won over 10 marketing, business and coaching industry awards.

CORPORATE CLIENTS HAVE INCLUDED:
Telstra, International Rice Research Institute, Wesfarmers, Amadeus, Virgin Australia, IKEA, LEGO, Mercedes-Benz, Australian Medical Association, Shell Energy and Workcover.

Book in a time to chat here:
https://calendly.com/jane-0877/complimentary-discussion
or Email: support@jane-anderson.com.au
Call the office: +61 7 3841 7772

Alternatively jump on Jane's website at **www.jane-anderson.com.au** to find out about her workshops, speaking and coaching programs.

JOIN THE WOMEN WITH INFLUENCE COMMUNITY

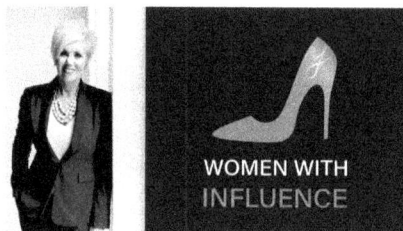

Grow your revenue by over $250,000 within 12 months.
Increase your confidence, presence and influence working with large organisations.

After having so many female corporate consultants asking Jane for advice on how to sell five, six and seven-figure programs and grow their corporate consulting practices, the Women with Influence Community was founded in 2017. It is Australia's leading community for female corporate consultants to become exceptional advisors.

Women have joined from all walks of life who want to grow their practices by selling their programs to large organisations, such as those who are featured in this book. From selling to retail billionaires to companies like eBay and Amazon, Jane's vision was to create a community of women to connect and collaborate, a place she wished she had when growing her own consulting practice.

Members are experts in areas such as:

- Leadership
- Resilience
- High performance
- Mindset

- Team effectiveness
- Cultural Transformation
- Goal Setting
- Career Success

Jane works with leading female corporate consultants in small intensive groups or one-on-one to help them to grow their practices with consistency and momentum. She has been featured on *Sky Business*, *Sunrise*, *The Today Show*, *The Age* and in the *Sydney Morning Herald*. She has worked with more than 25 different industries and spoken on stages to over 100,000 people.

To find out more go to **www.womenwithinfluence.com.au**.

READ MORE OF JANE'S WORK

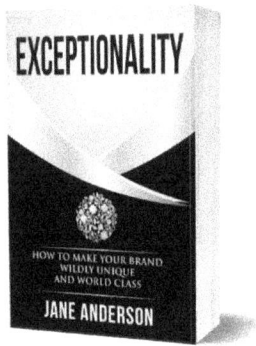

Have you ever wondered what makes some people have that certain 'chutzpah' that others don't?

Those who people describe as 'exceptional' are in all fields, from business to the arts, and from science to music. However, they all have a certain appeal that can be hard to both articulate and emulate.

Whether you want to be known as an exceptional person, personal brand, leader, team or business, in this book you will uncover the keys to elevating your influence, setting the standard and standing out from the crowd.

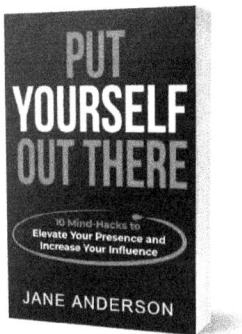

There used to be a saying that 'good things come to those who wait', but times have changed.

The pace of change, the rise of social media, video, podcasting and the ability to create your own platforms have meant our access to information and the ability to get in front of the right people has exploded.

Whether you want to work with dream clients, ask someone on a date, apply for that job, share your ideas or create a social following, Jane shares the top 10 mind hacks that she has used with thousands of clients to help them find the courage to put themselves out there. Now you can use them too.

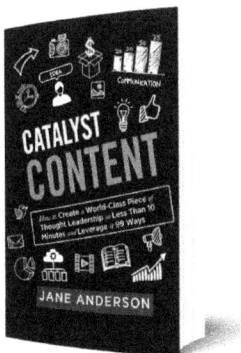

By the end of 2021 the content marketing industry will have grown to a $412 billion dollar industry from just $156 billion in 2015.

The rate of growth in content consumption has been dramatic and there's a risk that we're starting to create noise over value.

In this book Jane talks about the power of thought leadership and how to put your ideas out there. She discusses how to become prolific by creating the cadence of catalyst content that drives change.

This book is ideal for thought leaders, content creators and consultants looking to improve the quality and consistency of their thought leadership and content creation.

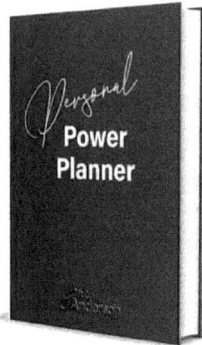

Did you know you're 40% more likely to achieve your goals if you write them down? That research led me to custom design this Personal Power Planner so it helps you stay aligned with your plan every day.

- Premium quality 100-page daily planner.

- Designed to help you focus and stay aligned with your vision and goals – every day.

- Simple, effective approach to managing time so you get your work done.

- Includes a video guide on how to use your Personal Power Planner to elevate your time management and achieve your goals.

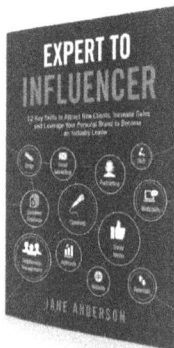

The old ways of growing a business have changed.

Social media has levelled the playing field and now it's easier than ever to compete with the big players in your industry.

Whether you're a thought leader, trusted advisor, academic or expert, the way you position and market yourself is now more important than ever.

This book will help you uncover the 12 secret activities to grow your business and opportunities.

Never has there been an opportunity for businesses and consultants to identify, engage and connect with their ideal audience like there is now with LinkedIn.

By the end of this book, you will have the strategies you need to generate leads and grow your business using LinkedIn. You will be armed with practical steps that you can implement straight away to see real results. Your outcomes will be stronger, and you will lead the competition on this new playing field.

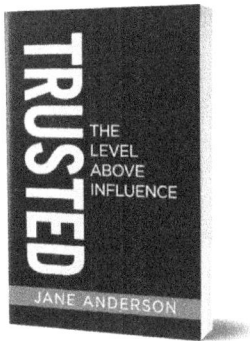

In a world of disruption and constant change, we've become more transparent than ever. Organisations and their leaders at all levels are challenged with adapting to changing customer demands, leading growth and attracting and retaining great talent. They're being asked to be more transparent, authentic and credible than ever.

In this sea of noise, when customers and employees are trying to make sense of so much change, they connect with those they trust.

In this book, Jane covers the nine key skills of high trust brands and global influencers that lead with influence and communicate during change.

We're no longer in the industrial or information age. We're now in the connection economy, where your ability to stand out, connect with others and position yourself in your career and business means security. It means you won't be left behind but instead be ahead of the pack.

Companies and governments no longer want people who want jobs for life. They want innovation, ideas and networks to thrive in volatile economic times. We are bombarded with information and choices every day. Hard work alone doesn't cut it anymore.

Discover how to create 'corporation you' without being a tall poppy to build your personal brand.

www.ingramcontent.com/pod-product-compliance
Lightning Source LLC
Chambersburg PA
CBHW051754200326
41597CB00025B/4557